by William Gibson

WINTER CROOK (*poems*)

DINNY AND THE WITCHES (*play*)

A CRY OF PLAYERS (*play*)

THE COBWEB (*novel*)

TWO FOR THE SEESAW (*play*)

THE SEESAW LOG (*chronicle*)

THE MIRACLE WORKER (*play*)

A MASS FOR THE DEAD (*chronicle & poems*)

AMERICAN PRIMITIVE (*play*)

A SEASON IN HEAVEN (*chronicle*)

THE BODY & THE WHEEL (*play*)

THE BUTTERFINGERS ANGEL, MARY & JOSEPH, HEROD THE NUT, & THE SLAUGHTER OF 12 HIT CAROLS IN A PEAR TREE (*play*)

GOLDA (*play*)

SHAKESPEARE'S GAME (*criticism*)

with Clifford Odets

GOLDEN BOY (*musical*)

Shakespeare's Game

William Gibson

SHAKESPEARE'S
GAME

Atheneum   *New York*   1978

Library of Congress Cataloging in Publication Data

Gibson, William, 1914–
    Shakespeare's game.

    1. Shakespeare, William, 1564–1616—Technique.
I. Title.
PR2995.G5   822.3'3   77-15912
ISBN 0-689-10877-x

Published simultaneously in Canada by McClelland and Stewart, Ltd.
Manufactured by American Book–Stratford Press,
Saddle Brook, New Jersey
Designed by Harry Ford
First Edition

in memoriam
CLIFFORD ODETS

1.	*Preliminary*	3
2.	*The Happening*	6
3.	*The Move, and Its Promise*	9
4.	*The Exposition*	13
5.	*Aside*	21
6.	*The Scene*	24
7.	*The Spring at the Center*	43
8.	*The Barrier*	54
9.	*The Body on the Skeleton*	56
10.	*Aside*	68
11.	*The Third-Act Pivot*	71
12.	*Double Plot, Comic*	77
13.	*Surrogates*	87
14.	*Double Plot, Tragic*	91
15.	*Aside*	113
16.	*The Inner Contradiction*	121
17.	*Consecutivity*	139
18.	*Unfinished Business*	149
19.	*The Plunge, Comic*	151
20.	*Aside*	173
21.	*The Moveless Sea*	176
22.	*The Plunge, Tragic*	188
23.	*Afterword*	219
	Index	225

Shakespeare's Game

I. *Preliminary*

I taught a graduate seminar in playwriting at one of our universities for two and a half years and stopped when I stopped learning in it, a good idea for any teacher. But I had other reasons to stop, and one was that the theatre I had written for was giving up the ghost while we talked, to a dirge of musical-comedy ditties, and the new theatre my students were to venture into was dispensing with playwrights altogether; I sometimes felt I was teaching a craft about as viable as whale harpooning.

Generation after generation the theatre has been on its death-bed—one of O'Neill's childhood memories was of his father telling him, "The theatre is dying"—which is another way of saying its class basis is changing. It never gets buried. The competition of film and television has been devastating, but these are costly media, in both money and integrity; theatre can be made under a streetlamp by three youngsters of talent without a cent, of whom there is an irrepressible supply, and it is the medium they will always begin in and renew.

3

This tide of new talent, new audiences, new styles is hard on the oldsters, who feel beached, and bid the sea back with much wailing against its ignorance. I was twice as old as my students, and wondered about my relevance. I told them of Marshal Foch, the 1918 savior of France, who subsequently instructed young officers in the war college, "This is what I did, and it worked; you must always do the same," whereupon the 1940 army was wiped out in six days. The students thought the parable funny, but my diffidence was an indulgence they soon disabused me of; they were starving, even for old-fashioned crumbs.

University theatre is in many respects admirable, and for most acting and directing students it is closer to the working theatre than they will ever again get, but even harpooning cannot be taught by someone who has never hit a whale. These were playwrights in their twenties, reasonably gifted and mature, on the verge of being stamped "masters," and none of them knew what a scene was. The question of whether playwriting can be taught at all hardly requires an answer: of course not, can you teach someone to be talented whom you can't even teach to be interesting? What you hope to teach is how to avoid being maximally boring. The first business of the writer in the theatre is to keep the audience from walking out, and that is the craft, and its ways are communicable in logical discussion; what lies beyond it is art, and up to God. Fashions in the theatre change with each generation like hair styles, but hair is hair, and I did not really believe that the strategies which had served great playwrights for twenty-five hundred years had been outgrown in the last ten by my young students. I

4

could at least teach them what a scene was, and as a first lesson I brought in one from that old killer of whales, Shakespeare.

Who never failed me, or them. I had no text to work from, with these students, other than their own scripts page by page, and when it was pertinent to some tangle in them I brought in work by our betters, dead and living; but I need never have looked beyond Shakespeare, who knew everything. I had been taken aback, when I first returned to him after myself becoming a playwright, to discover how modern he was: the problems of structure we were struggling with on Broadway were the very ones he was solving, in scene after scene, four hundred years ago. Those problems have not changed. Or it may be truer to say that, so potent has been his influence on the craft, his solutions have sired the problems we inherit; only in our time is there an effort to see a different set, and their fate is uncertain. And in a time when so much is uncertain—the disarray in our arts is of course a symptom—it may be of value to look again at the cornerstones of a most fecund tradition.

So:

2. *The Happening*

A play begins when a world in some state of equipoise, always uneasy, is broken into by a happening. Since it is not equipoise we have paid to see, but the loosing and binding of an evening's disorder, the sooner the happening the better; these plays open fast.

In *Hamlet*, after twenty lines we know we are waiting for a midnight "thing" to appear, and so it does after another twenty, the dumb ghost which "bodes some strange eruption to our state." In *Measure for Measure*, whose theme—"of government the properties to unfold" —is announced in its third line, we hear before the twentieth that the Duke has named his admired Angelo to serve as ruler in his absence, and "What figure of us think you he will bear?" In *King Lear*, a terse chat is interrupted by Lear's entrance, and his fourth sentence is, "Know that we have divided in three our kingdom" with "intent to shake all cares and business from our age."

It is each of these happenings which precipitates the play. Horatio promptly moves to tell young Hamlet of the ghost, which opens the eruption; the Duke a minute after his question takes his leave, which makes way for the answer; Lear in fifteen speeches disowns Cordelia, banishes Kent, and throws himself upon the mercies of the serpent's tooth—"a thankless child"—which begins gnawing at his intent.

A play is an energy system, and the business of the precipitating event is to introduce a disequilibrium, that is, to release energy. Characterization, language, mood and tempo, meaning, all the other attributes which will give the play its identity, wait upon that release; it animates them, they cannot begin to exist without it. And once begun, the "play" is that of contradictory energies working to arrive at a new equilibrium, if it kills everybody.

If it does not, it is a comedy; but we need not foresee this in the happening. The whimsical Duke conducts us into the bowels of despair at the edge of death, and the mad old King in earlier and later versions lives happily ever after. What matters in the happening is not so much the quality as the quantity of play it releases. It touches the spring at the center.

So the first scene of *The Tempest* gives us a sinking ship and several noblemen in consternation; this happening will deliver them into Prospero's hand for the first time, it upsets an equilibrium of twelve years. *Romeo and Juliet* gives us a street brawl between two feuding families, quelled by the Prince's decree that in any future disturbance "Your lives shall pay the forfeit"; this happening introduces a mortal peril into the social life of town, and under it Romeo goes masked to the house of his enemies and falls in love with their daughter. *The Merchant of Venice* gives us a wealthy shipowner seek-

7

ing a loan at interest—"I'll break a custom"—to subsidize the courtship of a friend; this happening both implicates him in the contract for a pound of his flesh, which one suspects was not originally to be taken anywhere "nearest his heart," and leads us to the lady who will extricate him from it.

If the happening has impact in itself—a ghost at midnight makes a certain claim on our attention—so much sooner will we join in the play. It is hardly by chance that so many openings are violent. The playwright who was my teacher said he liked to open a play "with a fight" because it awoke not only the audience's interest but his own. Yet the energies set loose must suffice for the evening, and they come not from the happening, however brisk—they lurk in that world which antecedes the happening. It is still unknown to us; and the playwright, with our attention on the perk, now must expose it to us.

So, exposition.

3. The Move, and Its Promise

Or not quite. The play has begun its movement, and its exposition is the next item on the playwright's agenda; but on ours the next is a look at the nature of the movement itself—which is unique, it differentiates drama from other literature.

It is as in chess, also an energy system, one move provokes another. Horatio, once he has seen the ghost, must act; the move is his. It requires a decision, and he can decide his eyes are failing and go off to the oculist, or the Denmark fog is too much and go south for the winter, but these decisions will take him and us into a different game, not too inviting. In truth, he has no choice, the one decision that moves this game forward is

> Let us impart what we have seen tonight
> Unto young Hamlet; for, upon my life,
> This spirit, dumb to us, will speak to him.

This move, bracketing the past event with one to come, is also a promise. Indeed, the promise here is of three to come, Horatio's meeting with Hamlet, Hamlet's with the ghost, and the ghost's tale; all the promises will be kept. The play is now on the mainline tracks, and its next stop must be at Hamlet himself.

In the Vienna of *Measure* things are wobblier. Off goes our whimsical Duke, leaving no move onstage; so, off goes everybody else, and we must begin again—in scene two. Ostensibly it is Angelo's move, and he makes it, but offstage, arresting Claudio for fornication. It is quasi, it promises nothing, and is in fact the concluding half of the precipitating event; the first decision made onstage is Claudio's, in sending for his sister to

> make friends
> To the strict deputy; bid herself assay him:
> I have great hope in that—

a true move, it promises us Isabella, and her great scene with Angelo which takes us into the heart of the play. But we revert to the Duke, looking for a monk's cowl in which to spy, because Angelo

> scarce confesses
> That his blood flows, or that his appetite
> Is more to bread than stone: hence shall we see,
> If power change purpose, what our seemers be.

And not until Isabella responds to her brother's message —"I will about it straight"—is the play in high gear. The wobble is an adumbration: the center of this play, now in Angelo, now in Isabella, now in the Duke, is as itinerant as its tone is ambiguous, and we call it "dark comedy" as a euphemism for not truly agreeing to so bumpy a ride.

No wobbling for Lear, that center is like the earth's, but there is much shuffling of the cards—all games are energy systems—before the first move is dealt. Half mad to begin with, parceling out his lands in ratio to his daughters' blarney, the old man is brought up by a decision not his:

LEAR   Now, our joy,
   . . . . what can you say to draw
   A third more opulent than your sisters? Speak.
CORDELIA   Nothing, my lord.
LEAR   Nothing!
CORDELIA   Nothing.
LEAR   Nothing will come of nothing: speak again.
CORDELIA   . . . . Why have my sisters husbands, if they say
   They love you all?

Cordelia's is half a move, a response, but no promise; and this is not her play, Lear at once pre-empts it to

> disclaim all my paternal care,
> Propinquity and property of blood,
> And as a stranger to my heart and me
> Hold thee from this for ever,

and dowers the others with her share. It is a second decision and still no promise, it simply closes the subject. Where are we headed?—out of the theatre, except that Kent is on hand to reopen negotiations with a third decision, his protest in the teeth of Lear's warning—

LEAR   Come not between the dragon and his wrath.
KENT   . . . . Revoke thy doom;
   Or, whilst I can vent clamour from my throat,
   I'll tell thee thou dost evil—

and again Lear overrides it with his own:

> Hear me, recreant!
> . . . . if on the tenth day following

II

> Thy banish'd trunk be found in our dominions,
> The moment is thy death. Away!

These four decisions are half-moves, pregnant with the play to come, we know all is astir, but its direction is promised only at the scene's end; the half-moves are used to precipitate it. Cordelia warns her sisters—and us—"I know you what you are," prays them to "use well our father," and leaves them to put their heads together; they are threatened, and not unreasonably, by the old man's fitful temper:

> GONERIL ... let's hit together. ...
> REGAN We shall further think on 't.
> GONERIL We must do something, and i' the heat.

Now we know the enemy, which is also to say, the direction; the true move has come, Goneril is next seen instructing her steward to bring Lear to heel.

We must do something, and i' the heat. The pulse of each play is in such moves; without them it is, if not lifeless, prostrate and in dubious health. They are the technical means, the spurts, of its movement from past to future, and the material between is either a consequence of or a preparation for them. Whatever the glories between, when cuts are made for actual performance, these moves are untouchable; minus any, the play would not be followable. And in each move the promise —of Hamlet and the ghost, of Isabella and Angelo, of Goneril and Lear—is a promise of discord.

Does the dramaturgic fact of the move imply an image of man himself? Of course, and it will emerge as the structure of the whole is elaborated.

4. *The Exposition*

To acquaint us with the past and to intimate the future, while intriguing us in the present, is the business of the exposition; the playwright is writing simultaneously in three tenses. It is the most tangled stretch of the play, and at his best he insinuates us deftly through it. Not at his best, he plods. We first looked at the move, because whether or not he has in hand a move to take us through is what makes the difference.

In the second scene of *The Tempest* we are put in possession of a great chunk of the past by the simplest means, narration. We have witnessed a shipwreck; and Prospero, to let us know who was aboard, sits Miranda down—

PROSPERO   'Tis time
    I should inform thee farther. . . .
    My brother, and thy uncle, call'd Antonio,—
    I pray thee, mark me,—that a brother should
    Be so perfidious!—he whom, next thyself,
    Of all the world I loved, and to him put
    The manage of my state; as at that time
    Through all the signories it was the first,

And Prospero the prime duke, being so reputed
In dignity, and for the liberal arts
Without a parallel; those being all my study,
The government I cast upon my brother,
And to my state grew stranger, being transported
And rapt in secret studies. Thy false uncle—
Dost thou attend me?

MIRANDA   Sir, most heedfully.

PROSPERO   Being once perfected how to grant suits,
How to deny them—

and perseveres, but with misgivings every ten lines:

PROSPERO   . . . . that now he was
The ivy which had hid my princely trunk,
And suck'd my verdure out on 't. Thou attend'st not.

MIRANDA   O, good sir, I do.

PROSPERO   I pray thee, mark me.
I, thus neglecting worldly ends, all dedicated
To closeness and the bettering of my mind
With that which, but by being so retired,
O'er-prized all popular rate, in my false brother
Awaked an evil nature; and my trust,
Like a good parent, did beget of him
A falsehood in its contrary, as great
As my trust was; which had indeed no limit,
A confidence sans bound. He being thus lorded,
Not only with what my revenue yielded,
But what my power might else exact, like one
Who having into truth, by telling of it,
Made such a sinner of his memory,
To credit his own lie, he did believe
He was indeed the duke; out o' the substitution,
And executing the outward face of royalty,
With all prerogative:—hence his ambition growing,—
Dost thou hear?

MIRANDA   Your tale, sir, would cure deafness.

14

Maybe. It goes on for another eighty lines, concluding on a note of compassion—

> Thou art inclined to sleep; 'tis a good dulness,
> And give it way: I know thou canst not choose—

and "Miranda sleeps," joining us. The playwright is hacking his way through the tangle—and knows it, Prospero's misgivings are his—because the narrative can provoke no move from Miranda; it is only for us, it has no consequence onstage. Our author is working only in two tenses, past and present, and the tale is dull, the scene is inactive, Miranda as a character is a cipher. Introduce a move for her—say that, hearing, she must fall upon her father with her fists—and how differently Prospero would offer his data: now the tale is give and take, but with that one move everything would be altered, the scene, the characters, their past and future, the play itself.

The difference is seen in another narrative, the ghost's in *Hamlet*, where a move in the listener onstage is obligatory; but we must dig into the exposition in the first act entire, which is perfection.

It begins at once, but as parenthetical matter between the ghost's two appearances when our curiosity is alert— Horatio explains "the source of this our watch" as the military threat from Fortinbras; then the ghost returns, they strike at it until it vanishes, and Horatio is off to young Hamlet. The opening scene is a prelude, agile, mysterious, and to the point, aimed at the main character and motive of the play.

The charge of its promise overhangs the next scene, and while we are suspended with it the playwright has our consent to introduce past material, inert at present, but necessary to future moves. The immediate promise must be kept, of course: Horatio cannot promise us Hamlet and give us the oculist instead. But once it is kept our appetite is satisfied, which is no better. The playwright's task therefore is to smuggle in new promises before he discharges the old, and the old must itself breed a greater.

So, in scene two, we wait for Horatio with our eye on young Hamlet in the court. The King speaks of his marriage to his dead brother's queen, dispatches messengers to forestall Fortinbras, and gives Laertes leave to sail for France; all this matter will be used, but when he turns to Hamlet the Queen joins him in chiding her son for "unmanly grief," and the basic triangle of the play is set. Hamlet is left alone for the first of the soliloquies which reveal the thoughts he cannot share—

> O, that this too too solid flesh would melt,
> Thaw and resolve itself into a dew!
> Or that the Everlasting had not fix'd
> His canon 'gainst self-slaughter!—

a suicidal despair which is not merely grief, it is rage at the triangle—

> Frailty, thy name is woman!—
> A little month, or ere those shoes were old
> With which she follow'd my poor father's body,
> Like Niobe, all tears:—why she, even she,—
> O God! a beast, that wants discourse of reason
> Would have mourn'd longer,—married with mine uncle, ...
> It is not, nor it cannot come to good—

16

and a spring of great promise has been set. It is into this coiled tension that Horatio now comes with his news of the ghost, and the immediate move passes to Hamlet:

> HAMLET   I will watch tonight;
>   Perchance 'twill walk again.
> HORATIO   I warrant it will.
> HAMLET   If it assume my noble father's person,
>   I'll speak to it, though hell itself should gape
>   And bid me hold my peace.

The promise, kept, *has* bred a greater; and Hamlet in a closing scrap of soliloquy enlarges it ominously:

> My father's spirit in arms! all is not well;
> I doubt some foul play: would the night were come!

The promise of what the night will bring now overhangs the act, and is potent enough that the playwright can sidle into other characters. The third scene introduces the one principal we have not met, Ophelia, bidding Laertes farewell; since he will not be back until the fourth act, here we must also make his further acquaintance simply to remember him; and he will come crying, "Give me my father," so that bond too must be manifest. But four birds in the hand are better than these three:

> LAERTES   For Hamlet, and the trifling of his favour,
>   Hold it. . . .
>   The perfume and suppliance of a minute;
>   No more.
> OPHELIA   No more but so?
> LAERTES   . . . fear it, my dear sister,
>   And keep you in the rear of your affection,
>   Out of the shot and danger of desire.

17

Polonius, having sent Laertes off with his fatherly blessing, pursues the topic:

POLONIUS   What is 't, Ophelia, he hath said to you?

OPHELIA   So please you, something touching the Lord Hamlet. . . .

POLONIUS   What is between you? give me up the truth.

OPHELIA   He hath, my lord, of late made many tenders
Of his affection to me.

POLONIUS   Affection! . . . .
I would not, in plain terms, from this time forth,
Have you so slander any moment leisure,
As to give words or talk with the Lord Hamlet.

And another promise has been wound. To set these characters in place for the moves to come is an obvious necessity; but to do so in terms of the absent Hamlet is a rich
economy, keeping him in the foreground and coloring
them with his reflected light, while moving forward in
a scene inherently static. Parenthetic to the larger promise, the placement of this scene is unerring; transplant it
to open the play—or to any other slot in the act—and it is
fatal to the movement.

Now the night comes. Scenes four and five on the
castle platform are in fact one scene, broken only to get
rid of Horatio and Marcellus for Hamlet's tête-à-tête
with the ghost. Waiting, Hamlet speaks of his uncle's
wassailing, that we may have that character in mind, and
we catch a premonitory glimpse of his own:

HAMLET   . . . . these men,—
Carrying, I say, the stamp of one defect,
Being nature's livery, or fortune's star,—
Their virtues else—be they as pure as grace. . . .
Shall in the general censure take corruption
From that particular fault. . . .

18

HORATIO   Look, my lord, it comes!
HAMLET   Angels and ministers of grace defend us!
. . . . What may this mean,
That thou, dead corse, again, in complete steel,
Revisit'st thus the glimpses of the moon,
Making night hideous . . .
Say, why is this? wherefore? what should we do?

Something, and i' the heat; it is the difference which makes the ghost's tale drama, and Prospero's narrative. The ghost beckons, and Hamlet breaks from the clutches of his companions to follow to "another part of the platform," where his question is answered at once:

HAMLET   Speak: I am bound to hear.
GHOST   So art thou to revenge, when thou shalt hear.
HAMLET   What?
GHOST   . . . List, list, O, list!
If thou didst ever thy dear father love—
HAMLET   O God!
GHOST   Revenge his foul and most unnatural murder.

So, his move defined for us, Hamlet hears the tale of his mother's adultery with his uncle and the poisoning of his father, which has the further interest of gossip about persons we have already met; and he accepts the move.

GHOST   But, howsoever thou pursuest this act,
Taint not thy mind, nor let thy soul contrive
Against thy mother aught. . . .
Adieu, adieu, adieu! remember me.

Exit

HAMLET   . . . . Remember thee!
Yea, from the table of my memory
I'll wipe away all trivial fond records, ...
And thy commandment all alone shall live
Within the book and volume of my brain,

> Unmix'd with baser matter. . . .
> I have sworn 't.

When Horatio and Marcellus find him he greets them with "but wild and whirling words," swears them to secrecy—with reason, the revelation has put his own life in danger—and the act ends; the exposition is complete.

The three moves underlying it are simple enough—Horatio informs Hamlet, Hamlet seeks out the ghost, the ghost enjoins Hamlet to revenge—but each has lifted the play to a new level of tautness from which it cannot be allowed to fall back. They accomplish the triple task of the exposition. First, they keep it in movement, that is, intrigue us in the present. Second, they draw into that movement more than a dozen characters to acquaint us with all the tensions of the world which antecedes the ghost, and with these onstage to drive the play the past tense can be dropped; henceforth the movement is in the clear and forward. Third, and crucially, they intimate its future.

In a word, the exposition has discovered the two antagonists; this is its main task, and it carries us to the threshold of the central action. Hamlet's closing couplet—

> The time is out of joint: O cursed spite,
> That ever I was born to set it right!—

is the promise which overhangs the rest of the play. As always, it is a promise of conflict: here, outwardly—"to set it right"—one between Hamlet and the King, and inwardly—"that ever I was born"—one in Hamlet himself. And with the term conflict, we have come within sight of the spring at the center.

5. *Aside*

So far we have followed Shakespeare's layout of a play—precipitating event, initial moves, exposition—with the eye of a first-night audience. It is time to enter a few qualifications, obvious enough, but better said.

First, the eye of that audience, deplore it as we may, is the fundamental condition of life in the theatre; and we are looking at the plays now as pieces of theatre craft. The minimal odds are ten thousand to one that an audience which emerges from a premiere yawning is sentencing the play to oblivion. To "hold the stage" means to hold the ticket buyers. It is no mean accomplishment, and Shakespeare expended as much care upon it as any modern writer of hit comedies. It required a hearty knowledge of his audience, that is, an intuition of their values and reactions; and the craft was his means of arousing, sustaining, and shaping their immediate response.

Clearly, there is a variety of audiences. But writers for an elite—from court masques to coffee-house skits—know theirs too; and the more homologous the audience, the less wide the net of the craft need be. Shakespeare's was the motley public, and that we are still to be counted among it is testimony to how deep his knowledge of us ran. The craft itself is part of his knowledge of us.

Second, it is patent that we return and return to his plays for other reasons. If the craft were only a bag of tricks to catch a wandering eye—which in part it is—it could be justified on a single count: the waste of so many great poets and novelists whose works for the stage accumulate dust in library stacks, because they would not learn the rudiments of the low trade Shakespeare spent his life in. A famous novelist said to me, "I think of the theatre as a Caribbean island, you go in on a pirate's raid and loot it." I said, "You won't make a cent," and he didn't; his play cost him a fortune to keep onstage a few weeks, a case of piracy in reverse. But the craft is not mere craft. It is, as we shall see, the playwright's touchstone of what goes in or is left out; it dictates the integrity of the play, is part of its beauty—the exposition in *Hamlet* has the shapeliness of a symphonic movement—and helps unlock in the playwright those illuminations of human experience which compel our subsequent returns. When I speak in such mechanical terms as the spring at the center, it is partly to distinguish the rational aspects of creativity from those which pass understanding; the distinction fails when craft becomes form. It is then inseparable from the art.

Third, the audience's eye takes in the play consecutively; it begins at the beginning, and moves to the center. The playwright's eye may begin at the end, or anywhere in the mental chaos which precedes his labors, and most of his early floundering is in quest of the center. It is the eye from the center, of course, which in rewriting elects the precipitating event and the moves of the exposition, imposing a retroactive logic upon it.

To Shakespeare, working from plots in texts under his hand, the center was discernible from the outset, one reason his colleagues "scarce received from him a blot in his papers." Given the center, however, he still had to erect a dramatic edifice around it; and now we must look at his building-block, the scene, whose structure will prefigure much of what we come to at the center.

6. The Scene

Like the move, the scene is unique to drama—though used sporadically in all story-telling—in being its very bonework. And we can define the scene only in terms of the move and its promise. It is that unit of time and place in which the move finds its object—which is the promise; one or the other is altered, if not both; and a new move is born of the encounter.

Thus the second scene of *Hamlet* opens on the object, Hamlet, whom we see Horatio's move find and alter—from "But break, my heart, for I must hold my tongue" to "I'll speak to it, though hell itself should gape"—and it ends on Hamlet's choice of move. The fourth-fifth scene opens on that move, which finds its object, the ghost, and is itself altered, becoming now the move to "set it right"—a considerable journey from "hold my tongue." We may note that is the psychological distance and depth of the alterations effected which take us beyond entertainment and into art.

The more resistant the object, the more potent is the new move born of the encounter; thus it is that the promise, kept, breeds a greater. In the exposition the object is relatively passive, and the scene is low in tension. But each move is an act of will; and its object, like Hamlet, is quickened to another act of will. Deeper in the play, the scene is redefinable then in terms not of move against object, but of will against will.

It is at its leanest between two characters; and the specimens we now dissect in detail are in essence two-character scenes, taken from one play, a chain of three links.

In the second act of *Measure for Measure*, Isabella leaves her nunnery and goes to Angelo's house; her move, to plead for a fornicator's life, is the given. The scene begins with an exchange between Angelo and the Provost of the prison—

PROVOST   Is it your will Claudio shall die tomorrow?
ANGELO   Did I not tell thee yea? hadst thou not order?
  Why dost thou ask again?
PROVOST   . . . . I have seen,
  When, after execution, Judgement hath
  Repented. . . .
ANGELO   Go to; let that be mine:
  Do you your office, or give up your place—

which gives us the object as immovable. The interest now is in the working-out of the two givens in collision. Isabella, ushered in, opens on a note of some revulsion which will be relevant much later:

ANGELO   Well; what's your suit?
ISABELLA   There is a vice that most I do abhor,
  And most desire should meet the blow of justice;
  For which I would not plead, but that I must;

> For which I must not plead, but that I am
> At war 'twixt will and will not.
> ANGELO   Well; the matter?
> ISABELLA   I have a brother is condemn'd to die:
> I do beseech you, let it be his fault,
> And not my brother.

It is her first—allow me the discrimination—submove, to separate the crime and criminal, and hardly irresistible; Angelo counters it so capably that she agrees:

> ANGELO   Condemn the fault, and not the actor of it?
> Why, every fault's condemn'd ere it be done:
> Mine were the very cipher of a function,
> To fine the faults whose fine stands in record,
> And let go by the actor.
> ISABELLA   O just but severe law!
> I had a brother, then.

And turning to leave is her second submove, which would abort the scene; but her escort, Claudio's friend, has his own miniature scene to play, with her as the object.

> LUCIO (*aside to Isab.*)   Kneel down before him, hang upon his gown:
> You are too cold; if you should need a pin,
> You could not with more tame a tongue desire it:
> To him, I say!
> ISABELLA   Must he needs die?
> ANGELO   Maiden, no remedy.
> ISABELLA   Yes: I do think that you might pardon him,
> And neither heaven nor man grieve at the mercy.

It is her next submove, an appeal to mercy in the abstract; but Angelo is indifferent even to her presence:

ANGELO   I will not do 't.

ISABELLA   But can you, if you would?

ANGELO   Look, what I will not, that I cannot do.

ISABELLA   But might you do 't, and do the world no wrong,
If so your heart were touch'd with that remorse
As mine is to him?

She is feeling her way—and Lucio will call our attention
to it, "touch *him*"—from the abstract to the personal;
with each submove she aims more at Angelo, the "deputed sword" and judge, equating him first with Claudio,
next with herself—

ANGELO   He's sentenced; 'tis too late.

ISABELLA   Too late? why no; I, that do speak a word,
May call it back again. . . .
Not the king's crown, nor the deputed sword,
The marshal's truncheon, nor the judge's robe,
Become them with one half so good a grace
As mercy does.
If he had been as you, and you as he,
You would have slipt like him; but he, like you,
Would not have been so stern.

ANGELO   Pray you, be gone.

ISABELLA   I would to heaven I had your potency,
And you were Isabel; should it then be thus?
No; I would tell what 'twere to be a judge,
And what a prisoner.

LUCIO (*aside to Isab.*)   Ay, touch him; there's the **vein**.

ANGELO   Your brother is a forfeit of the law,
And you but waste your words.

ISABELLA   Alas, alas!
Why, all the souls that were were forfeit once;
And He that might the vantage best have took
Found out the remedy. How would you be,
If He, which is the top of judgement, should
But judge you as you are?—

27

and hits the target. Angelo sees her at last, she is "fair," and he enters the argument, point counter point.

ANGELO   Be you content, fair maid;
  It is the law, not I condemn your brother:
  Were he my kinsman, brother, or my son,
  It should be thus with him. . . .
ISABELLA   Good, good my lord, bethink you;
  Who is it that hath died for this offence?
  There's many have committed it. . . .
ANGELO   The law hath not been dead, though it hath slept:
  Those many had not dared to do that evil,
  If the first that did the edict infringe
  Had answer'd for his deed; now 'tis awake,
  Takes note of what is done. . . .
ISABELLA   Yet show some pity.
ANGELO   I show it most of all when I show justice;
  For then I pity those I do not know,
  Which a dismiss'd offense would after gall;
  And do him right that, answering one foul wrong,
  Lives not to act another. . . .
ISABELLA   So you must be the first that gives his sentence,
  And he, that suffers. O, it is excellent
  To have a giant's strength; but it is tyrannous
  To use it like a giant.
LUCIO (*aside to Isab.*)   That's well said.

Indeed, and should be chiselled in the lobby of the United Nations.

ISABELLA   Could great men thunder
  As Jove himself does, Jove would ne'er be quiet,
  For every pelting, petty officer
  Would use his heaven for thunder.
  Nothing but thunder! Merciful Heaven,
  Thou rather with thy sharp and sulphurous bolt
  Split'st the unwedgeable and gnarled oak

28

Than the soft myrtle: but man, proud man,
Drest in a little brief authority,
Most ignorant of what he's most assured,
His glassy essence, like an angry ape,
Plays such fantastic tricks before high heaven
As make the angels weep; who, with our spleens,
Would all themselves laugh mortal.

LUCIO (*aside to Isab.*) O, to him, to him, wench! he will re-
lent;
He's coming; I perceive 't.

Angelo is silent now, all eyes—and who would not be, on
a girl who talks like *that?*—while she reminds him how
much is forgiven to the privileged. It kindles a doubt and
a fire in him, is she offering herself? until it is he who
must turn to leave:

ISABELLA Great men may jest with saints; 'tis wit in them,
But in the less foul profanation. . . .
That in the captain's but a choleric word,
Which in the soldier is flat blasphemy. . . .

ANGELO Why do you put these sayings upon me?

ISABELLA Because authority, though it err like others,
Hath yet a kind of medicine in itself,
That skins the vice o' the top. Go to your bosom;
Knock there, and ask your heart what it doth know
That's like my brother's fault. . . .

ANGELO (*aside*)   She speaks, and 'tis
Such sense, that my sense breeds with it. Fare you well.

ISABELLA Gentle my lord, turn back.

ANGELO I will bethink me: come again tomorrow.

ISABELLA Hark how I'll bribe you: good my lord, turn
back.

ANGELO How? bribe me?

But Isabella means only with "true prayers" by her sister
nuns.

ANGELO (*aside*)   Amen:
  For I am that way going to temptation,
  Where prayers cross.
ISABELLA   At what hour tomorrow
  Shall I attend your lordship?
ANGELO   At any time 'fore noon.

So, their scene but not their business concluded, Isabella leaves Angelo alone with what has opened in him:

What's this, what's this? Is this her fault or mine?
The tempter or the tempted, who sins most?
Ha!
Not she; nor doth she tempt: but it is I
That, lying by the violet in the sun,
Do as the carrion does, not as the flower,
Corrupt with virtuous season. . . .
What dost thou, or what art thou, Angelo?
Dost thou desire her foully for those things
That make her good? O, let her brother live:
Thieves for their robbery have authority
When judges steal themselves. What, do I love her,
That I desire to hear her speak again,
And feast upon her eyes? What is 't I dream on?
O cunning enemy, that, to catch a saint,
With saints dost bait thy hook!

It has taken a most interesting turn, what began as a struggle between two wills is now an inner struggle in one. The object has been altered, and a new move born, with a greater promise; the scene is accomplished—more, *proved*, with all the evidence visible. It has overturned their roles; and when they next meet Isabella will be the object, Angelo the suitor.

The new promise in their scene on the morrow is again a collision of two givens, likewise new, his desire and her

chastity. But Angelo's move is double, first against himself, then against Isabella; and still at stake is her brother's life, or her initial move. So each of the givens is
itself "at war 'twixt will and will not," and the working-
out is, in Angelo, tortuous.

The new scene opens on him alone, after a night with
his two alternatives—"several" means separate—

> When I would pray and think, I think and pray
> To several subjects. Heaven hath my empty words;
> Whilst my invention, hearing not my tongue,
> Anchors on Isabel: Heaven in my mouth,
> As if I did but only chew his name;
> And in my heart the strong and swelling evil
> Of my conception. . . . yea, my gravity,
> Wherein—let no man hear me—I take pride,
> Could I with boot change for an idle plume,
> Which the air beats for vain.

The scale dips further, into an exact physiology of what
we moderns call anxiety, the moment Isabella is announced:

ANGELO   O heavens!
  Why does my blood thus muster to my heart,
  Making both it unable for itself,
  And dispossessing all my other parts
  Of necessary fitness?
  So play the foolish throngs with one that swoons;
  Come all to help him, and so stop the air
  By which he should revive. . . .
                    Enter Isabella.
                              How now, fair maid?
ISABELLA   I am come to know your pleasure.
ANGELO   That you might know it, would much better
  please me
  Than to demand what 'tis.

The choice will not be actual until he says it; the flesh must be made word. Isabella takes the first of his inward recoils as conclusive:

> ANGELO   Your brother cannot live.
> ISABELLA   Even so.—Heaven keep your honour!

But the scene so concluded would outrage us; it is not the one promised, by either the playwright to us or Angelo to himself. So playwright and Angelo join to detain her.

> ANGELO   Yet may he live awhile; and, it may be,
>   As long as you or I: yet he must die.
> ISABELLA   Under your sentence?
> ANGELO   Yea.
> ISABELLA   When, I beseech you? . . . .
> ANGELO   Ha! fie, these filthy vices! It were as good
>   To pardon him that hath from nature stolen
>   A man already made, as to remit
>   Their saucy sweetness that do coin heaven's image
>   In stamps that are forbid. . . .
> ISABELLA   'Tis set down so in heaven, but not in earth.
> ANGELO   Say you so? then I shall pose you quickly.
>   Which had you rather,—that the most just law
>   Now took your brother's life; or, to redeem him,
>   Give up your body to such sweet uncleanness
>   As she that he hath stained?

It is only hypothetical, still in the balance between "sweet" and "uncleanness," and Isabella misunderstands him again and again while he flounders in subjunctives:

> ISABELLA   I had rather give my body than my soul.
> ANGELO   I talk not of your soul. . . .
>   Might there not be a charity in sin
>   To save this brother's life?

ISABELLA   Please you to do 't,
   I'll take it as a peril to my soul,
   It is no sin at all, but charity.
ANGELO   Pleased you to do't at peril of your soul,
   Were equal poise of sin and charity.
ISABELLA   That I do beg his life, if it be sin,
   Heaven let me bear it! you granting of my suit,
   If that be sin, I'll make it my morn prayer
   To have it added to the faults of mine. . . .
ANGELO   Your sense pursues not mine: either you are ig-
   norant,
   Or seem so, craftily; and that's not good.
ISABELLA   Let me be ignorant, and in nothing good,
   But graciously to know I am no better.
ANGELO   . . . . I'll speak more gross:
   Your brother is to die.
ISABELLA   So.
ANGELO   And his offence is so, as it appears,
   Accountant to the law upon that pain.
ISABELLA   True.
ANGELO   Admit no other way to save his life,—
   As I subscribe not that, nor any other,
   But in the loss of question,—that you, his sister,
   Finding yourself desired of such a person,
   Whose credit with the judge, or own great place,
   Could fetch your brother from the manacles
   Of the all-building law; and that there were
   No earthly mean to save him, but that either
   You must lay down the treasures of your body
   To this supposed, or else to let him suffer;
   What would you do?

No less iffy, this is unambiguous enough to move Isabella—still pleading for her brother—into her own war
'twixt will and will not. But the playwright chooses not
to open a second front; the note of sexual revulsion on

which Isabella first introduced herself is hurried into play:

> ISABELLA   . . . strip myself to death, as to a bed
>   That longing have been sick for, ere I'ld yield
>   My body up to shame.
> ANGELO   Then must your brother die.
> ISABELLA   And 'twere the cheaper way:
>   Better it were a brother died at once,
>   Than that a sister, by redeeming him,
>   Should die for ever.

Times change, and hopes of heaven with them; what the nineteenth century held dear as a portrait of woman at her most angelic today seems more like one of a born priss. But either way there is no cooperation in her—nor mercy, alas, now that its skin is off her ass—and Angelo, disappointed in every hint, must push on solo to the bitter and stammering end.

> ANGELO   Were you not, then, as cruel as the sentence
>   That you have slandered so?
> ISABELLA   . . . . lawful mercy
>   Is nothing kin to foul redemption.
> ANGELO   You seem'd of late to make the law a tyrant;
>   And rather proved the sliding of your brother
>   A merriment than a vice.
> ISABELLA   O, pardon me, my lord. . . .
>   I something do excuse the thing I hate,
>   For his advantage that I dearly love.
> ANGELO   We are all frail.
> ISABELLA   Else let my brother die. . . .
> ANGELO   Nay, women are frail too.
> ISABELLA   Ay, as the glasses where they view themselves;
>   Which are as easy broke as they make forms. . . .
> ANGELO   And from this testimony of your own sex,—
>   Since, I suppose, we are made to be no stronger

34

Than faults may shake our frames,—let me be bold;—
I do arrest your words. Be that you are,
That is, a woman; if you be more, you're none;
If you be one,—as you are well express'd
By all external warrants,—show it now,
By putting on the destined livery.
ISABELLA   I have no tongue but one. . . .
ANGELO   Plainly conceive, I love you.

So Angelo achieves his move, and is committed to it;
now all is outward, and the dénouement is swift. The
move passes to Isabella—

ISABELLA   I know your virtue hath a license in't,
Which seems a little fouler than it is,
To pluck on others.
ANGELO   Believe me, on mine honour,
My words express my purpose.
ISABELLA   Ha! . . . Seeming, seeming!—
I will proclaim thee, Angelo; look for't;
Sign me a present pardon for my brother,
Or with an outstretch'd throat I'll tell the world aloud
What man thou art—

and thus passes back to Angelo, whose "appetite" is
surely made more "sharp" by humiliation—

ANGELO   Who will believe thee, Isabel?
My unsoil'd name, the austereness of my life,
My vouch against you, and my place i' the state,
Will so your accusation overweigh,
That you shall stifle in your own report,
And smell of calumny. I have begun;
And now I give my sensual race the rein:
Fit thy consent to my sharp appetite;
. . . . redeem thy brother
By yielding up thy body to my will;
Or else he must not only die the death,

35

But thy unkindness shall his death draw out
To lingering sufferance. Answer me tomorrow,
Or, by the affection that now guides me most,
I'll prove a tyrant—

—and so, with his vengeful departure, passes back to Isabella.

Here the move has found its object—not without labor, despite their prior appointment—and each has altered the other. Angelo, compounding lust with injustice, is risking his place i' the state; Isabella, come for simple news, ends up clutching her chastity to her. The scene is almost done. It lacks only the element of further promise, a new move; and the playwright will not let Isabella leave the stage until she divulges it.

I'll to my brother:
. . . . had he twenty heads to tender down
On twenty bloody blocks, he'd yield them up,
Before his sister should her body stoop
To such abhorr'd pollution.

Which we, of course, take as rather too good to be true; our interest now is turned to Claudio, the new object, and Isabella's new move to

. . . tell him yet of Angelo's request,
And fit his mind to death. . . .

In Claudio's cell, our third scene, she is anticipated in this by the "Duke of dark corners," skulking about as a monk; his brief exchange with the condemned man— brief at least on Claudio's side—prefaces the scene proper. The body of their exchange is another stretch of the superb talk which marks this chain of scenes:

CLAUDIO   I've hope to live, and am prepared to die.
DUKE   Be absolute for death; either death or life
   Shall thereby be the sweeter. Reason thus with life:
   If I do lose thee, I do lose a thing
   That none but fools would keep: a breath thou art,
   Servile to all the skyey influences,
   That dost this habitation, where thou keep'st,
   Hourly afflict: merely, thou art death's fool;
   For him thou labour'st by thy flight to shun,
   And yet runn'st toward him still. Thou art not noble;
   For all the accommodations that thou bear'st
   Are nursed by baseness. Thou'rt by no means valiant;
   For thou dost fear the soft and tender fork
   Of a poor worm. Thy best of rest is sleep,
   And that thou oft provokest; yet grossly fear'st
   Thy death, which is no more. Thou art not thyself;
   For thou exist'st on many a thousand grains
   That issue out of dust. Happy thou art not;
   For what thou hast not, still thou strivest to get,
   And what thou hast, forget'st. Thou art not certain;
   For thy complexion shifts to strange effects,
   After the moon. If thou art rich, thou'rt poor;
   For, like an ass whose back with ingots bows,
   Thou bear'st thy heavy riches but a journey,
   And death unloads thee. Friend hast thou none;
   For thine own bowels, which do call thee sire,
   The mere effusion of thy proper loins,
   Do curse the gout, serpigo, and the rheum,
   For ending thee no sooner. Thou hast nor youth nor age,
   But, as it were, an after-dinner's sleep,
   Dreaming of both; for all thy blessed youth
   Becomes as aged, and doth beg the alms
   Of palsied eld; and when thou art old and rich,
   Thou hast neither heat, affection, limb, nor beauty,
   To make thy riches pleasant. What's yet in this
   That bears the name of life? Yet in this life

Lie hid moe thousand deaths: yet death we fear,
That makes these odds all even.

CLAUDIO   I humbly thank you.
To sue to live, I find I seek to die;
And, seeking death, find life: let it come on.

More than rhetoric, the passage is another miniature
scene in itself, and its tactical function is to firm up the
object, Claudio, as unalterable; his alteration when it
comes will thus travel a maximal distance. Which is to
say, evoke a maximal doubt and interest in the audience.

Left alone to begin, Isabella and Claudio are seemingly in accord. If true, there can be no scene—no alteration, no scene—but there is a sleeper in both move and
object. The latent content of Isabella's news is that it is
in her power to let Claudio live; the latent content of his
resoluteness leaks out in his first questions.

CLAUDIO   Is there no remedy?
ISABELLA   None, but such remedy as, to save a head,
    To cleave a heart in twain.
CLAUDIO   But is there any?
ISABELLA   Yes, brother, you may live:
    There is a devilish mercy in the judge,
    If you'll implore it, that will free your life,
    But fetter you till death.
CLAUDIO   Perpetual durance?
ISABELLA   Ay, just; perpetual durance, a restraint,
    Though all the world's vastidity you had,
    To a determined scope.
CLAUDIO   But in what nature?
ISABELLA   In such a one as, you consenting to't,
    Would bark your honour from that trunk you bear
    And leave you naked.
CLAUDIO   Let me know the point.

Isabella, now suspecting the twenty heads were a sisterly overestimation, suspends her move; and they exchange submoves in a subscene.

> ISABELLA   O, I do fear thee, Claudio; and I quake,
>   Lest thou a feverous life shouldst entertain,
>   And six or seven winters more respect
>   Than a perpetual honour. Darest thou die?
>   The sense of death is most in apprehension;
>   And the poor beetle, that we tread upon,
>   In corporal sufferance finds a pang as great
>   As when a giant dies.
> CLAUDIO   Why give you me this shame?
>   Think you I can a resolution fetch
>   From flowery tenderness? If I must die,
>   I will encounter darkness as a bride,
>   And hug it in mine arms.

So, with his unalterability firm again, Isabella is encouraged to complete her move:

> ISABELLA   If I would yield him my virginity,
>   Thou mightst be freed.
> CLAUDIO   O heavens; it cannot be.
> ISABELLA   . . . . This night's the time
>   That I should do what I abhor to name,
>   Or else thou diest tomorrow.
> CLAUDIO   Thou shalt not do 't.
> ISABELLA   O, were it but my life,
>   I'ld throw it down for your deliverance
>   As frankly as a pin.
> CLAUDIO   Thanks, dear Isabel.
> ISABELLA   Be ready, Claudio, for your death tomorrow.
> CLAUDIO   Yes.

A lovely girl, full of those high principles which also make the angels weep. Here the accord ends—and if this were all, the exchange would waste the precious minutes and footage of the stage; better a messenger running in to inform anyone in six words, Isabella told Claudio and he agrees. But now the sleeper in both move and object begins its work. Midway, the scene turns; the move becomes Claudio's and Isabella is the object.

CLAUDIO　　　　　Sure, it is no sin;
　Or of the deadly seven it is the least.
ISABELLA　Which is the least?
CLAUDIO　If it were damnable, he being so wise,
　Why would he for the momentary trick
　Be perdurably fined?—O Isabel!
ISABELLA　What says my brother?
CLAUDIO　　　　　　Death is a fearful thing.
ISABELLA　And shamed life a hateful.
CLAUDIO　Ay, but to die—

and here we get the underside of the Duke's coin—

CLAUDIO　Ay, but to die, and go we know not where;
　To lie in cold obstruction and to rot;
　This sensible warm motion to become
　A kneaded clod; and the delighted spirit
　To bathe in fiery floods, or to reside
　In thrilling region of thick-ribbed ice;
　To be imprison'd in the viewless winds,
　And blown with restless violence round about
　The pendent world; or to be worse than worst
　Of those that lawless and incertain thought
　Imagine howling:—'tis too horrible!
　The weariest and most loathed worldly life
　That age, ache, penury, and imprisonment
　Can lay on nature is a paradise
　To what we fear of death.
ISABELLA　Alas, alas!
CLAUDIO　　　　　　Sweet sister, let me live.

Whose move is it now?—Isabella's, and she repudiates his rebirth.

> ISABELLA   O dishonest wretch!
> Wilt thou be made a man out of my vice?
> Is't not a kind of incest, to take life
> From thine own sister's shame? . . .
> Die, perish!

But what if she did not?

It is a curious ending to the scene. Isabella's move has found and altered its object, Claudio, who in turn initiates his own move; but his neither alters her nor is altered. Thus no new move, or promise, can emerge. We end in an inertia, no one has anywhere further to go.

Yet a new move was in fact open—for Isabella, shaken by her brother's despair, to accept the rendezvous with Angelo—and the grain, the very existence, of the scene flows inexorably toward this reversal. Instead, the playwright at precisely this moment turns the play over to the Duke, who flogs it through the next three acts like a ringmaster of cruel monkeyshines, tricking everyone; tells Claudio he must die, produces out of his hat a cast-off fiancée of Angelo's to simulate Isabella in bed, sends another prisoner's head to Angelo as Claudio's, tells Isabella her brother is decapitated, condemns Angelo to the block and Lucio to the gallows, but all in fun, puts everything to rights, and in a climax of bad judgment marries Isabella himself. The decline of the play into this specious movement-by-mendacity, knotted merely to be unknotted, originates in the move not taken.

It is habitual to observe that Shakespeare improved on his sources. The sources here are an Italian tale and an English play based upon it, and in both we find Isabella leaving Claudio to keep the rendezvous with Angelo—indeed, begging the Duke later for Angelo's life. These would have been marvellous scenes to have in Shakespeare's hand. Clearly, his avoidance of them was deliberate, and chosen for some reason—the old audience wanted a new turn, or the repertoire needed a comedy of monkeyshines, or the actor for the Duke demanded a star part—which was good enough for a man of genius. It was just not good enough for this play.

So much for the classic scene, shaped from within by the urging of the move. It can catch up a dozen characters, but under the hubbub it must answer to the identical questioning: who has the move and who personifies the object? which is altered? what new move is the consequence? Passages not answerable to these questions are side-dishes, and had better be pretty tasty.

The move, however, transcends the scene. By its promise, kept, we mean that function of the move which couples to scene. In the chain of three here looked at, the new move born of the first scene—Angelo's lust—is what opens the second; the new move born of the second—Isabella's "fitting" Claudio for death—is what opens the third. In the case of double plots, scenes alternate and the moves play leapfrog. So the whole play is linked together, and carried forward—the edifice and its movement are synonymous. The new move not born of our third scene is what makes this play jump its tracks.

The move, we begin to suspect, is the microstructure which shapes all the structures of the work. It need not surprise us then if, like the scene, the central action—verily, the play itself—is definable in terms of the move.

7. *The Spring at the Center*

In the moment that the exposition discovers the two antagonists, one is seen as the move and the other as the object; the struggle between this move and object—or, two wills—is the central action of the play. Tragedy, history, or comedy.

When Hamlet accepts the ghost's charge to "revenge his . . . most unnatural murder" by the King, he takes upon himself the master move of the game, to "set it right"; the master object is the King. Whatever else intervenes, the crowning action must be a decisive encounter between Hamlet and the King. Much else does and must intervene. It would be conceivable for Hamlet to go directly to the King and stab him, but then we would have no game, and no Hamlet to explore; he would be Hotspur. The body of the play is thus a working-out of the intervening matter, which we shall look closely into later.

Throughout, the encounter which pends between Hamlet and the King is the master promise, or the spring at the center, from which everything else in the play derives its movement. Without it, the lesser characters—Hamlet's mother, Ophelia, Rosencrantz and Guildenstern, the actors, Polonius, Laertes—would have no business to interest us; it is the master promise which sets them too in motion. This promise is what we sometimes, and too simply, call "the" conflict.

In a looser "history," the First Part of *Henry IV*, the two antagonists do not meet face-to-face until the penultimate scene of the fifth act, and then for a mere minute. But in the opening scene they are adumbrated as opponents before either sets foot onstage; the King is envious

> that my Lord Northumberland
> Should be the father to so blest a son,
> Whilst I, by looking on the praise of him,
> See riot and dishonour stain the brow
> Of my young Harry. O that it could be proved
> That some night-tripping fairy had exchanged,
> In cradle-clothes our children where they lay. . . .
> Then would I have his Harry, and he mine,

so dreadful a wish for a father to utter that we are half-promised it will be cancelled out. The "happening" which precipitates the play is divided between this scene and the third, Hotspur's refusal to deliver his prisoners. The second scene uncovers Prince Hal at his shenanigans with Falstaff; in soliloquy at its end he resolves to

> pay the debt I never promised. . . .
> I'll so offend, to make offence a skill;
> Redeeming time when men think least I will.

and the cancelling-out *is* promised. In the third scene we find the other Harry, Hotspur, pledging himself to a "noble plot" against not only the King, but

>   that same sword-and-buckler Prince of Wales,
> But that I think his father loves him not
> And would be glad he met with some mischance,
> I'd have him poison'd with a pot of ale.

Thus in the exposition of this first act the two antagonists are postulated as move and object; the distinction here is finer, but Prince Hal as characterized has the choice of move, redemption. The master promise of their convergence overhangs the play. Whatever else intervenes, the crowning action must be a decisive encounter between Prince Hal and Hotspur; it has a poignance, both are delights, and there is no villain. It is almost a lovers' meeting.

The action proceeds by alternate scenes, featuring now the Prince, now Hotspur, in which each mocks and challenges the unmet other. So Prince Hal:

I am not yet of Percy's mind, the Hotspur of the north; he that kills me some six or seven dozen of Scots at a breakfast, washes his hands, and says to his wife, 'Fie upon this quiet life! I want work.'

And Hotspur:

>   Where is his son,
> The nimble-footed madcap Prince of Wales,
> And his comrades, that daff'd the world aside,
> And bid it pass? . . . . Come, let me taste my horse,
> Who is to bear me like a thunderbolt
> Against the bosom of the Prince of Wales:
> Harry to Harry—

And Prince Hal to his father:

>   I will redeem all this on Percy's head. . . .
>   And that shall be the day, whene'er it lights,

45

> That this same child of honour and renown,
> This gallant Hotspur, this all-praised knight,
> And your unthought-of Harry chance to meet.

And Hotspur:

> yet once ere night
> I will embrace him with a soldier's arm,
> That he shall shrink under my courtesy.

For four acts, by such promise after promise, their encounter is enhanced, exactly like the final "walkdown" between good guy and bad in a Western movie. Meanwhile, the lesser characters—Falstaff, if we dare call him lesser, Hotspur's wife, the King, Glendower, all entrancing in their own right—serve structurally as settings to bring out these two diamonds of honor, fated to collide. Indeed, the Prince "to save the blood" of war offers to meet Hotspur in single combat; but this violation of history is too much even for Shakespeare, and it is only in the ultimate confusion of battle that their minute comes, master move and object meet, and the Prince kills Hotspur.

Who actually died on that field of an anonymous arrow, two years after he and the Prince had shared the command of a Welsh campaign: art is much tidier than life with respect to a spring at the center.

Shall we try a pair of comedies?—on a single theme, love's follies, and both set in the inner forest where truth is hunted. In each we pursue a genuine lovers' meeting. The master promise implied in "boy meets girl, boy loses girl, boy gets girl"—the quote of course is taken from an American farce mocking the banalities of Hollywood

46

in the thirties—has animated every romantic comedy written; it is the spring at the center of both *A Midsummer-Night's Dream* and *As You Like It*.

The *Dream* moves on four levels of action, which interweave. The first is the pending marriage of Theseus and Hippolyta; it is without drama, and chiefly serves in the opening and concluding acts as a frame serves a picture. The second is the tangle of that foursome—it is a "twins" play without twins—whose names no one can keep straight from one page to another, Hermia and Lysander, Helena and Demetrius, who offer the master knot of the play. In the first scene we learn that Hermia loves Lysander; Lysander and Demetrius both love Hermia; Helena loves Demetrius. But Hermia's father insists she marry Demetrius. By Athenian law, passed perhaps just in time for this play, if Hermia disobeys she must either "die the death" or enter a nunnery to be

> a barren sister all your life,
> Chanting faint hymns to the cold fruitless moon.

This decree by Theseus is the "happening." Hermia's move is to run away instead with Lysander, and Helena curries favor with Demetrius by divulging it; we will next see this foursome in the forest. The second scene introduces the third level of action, with the artisans at work on the absurd play they will perform at Theseus' wedding. In the next scene we are in the forest, and the "dream" opens on the fourth level: Oberon and Titania are feuding in faeryland, and to humiliate her Oberon sends Puck after a magic flower, "love-in-idleness," whose juice

47

> on sleeping eye-lids laid
> Will make or man or woman madly dote
> Upon the next live creature that it sees.

"It"! In passing, to help Helena, Oberon asks Puck to dab the eyelids of Demetrius; Puck in a mistake of love's magic dabs Lysander, whose "next live creature" is the incredulous Helena—he has been telling her how odious she is—but Lysander observes sagely that

> The will of man is by his reason sway'd
> And reason says you are the worthier maid,

and thereafter the foursome go spinning through the forest like a top.

This material is complex, and some working-out on one level precedes some exposition on another; but on each level there is a move and an object, with one significant exception. The exception is structural, at the crux of the play, where its structure and its meaning are one.

On the first level, Theseus is the move, Hippolyta is the object, and the promise is their marriage, not that anyone cares. The master promise is on the second level, the disentanglement of the foursome; whatever else intervenes, the crowning action must be that. And is. But which of them has the move for it?—none, it is Oberon's, and from the fourth or supernatural level. Because the truth in this forest, the theme of the comedy, is savage: man's reason is a dream, and sexual pairing is maniacal. So even the immortal queen of faeryland, enamored of an ass, breathes upon him, "Thou art as wise as thou art beautiful." Perhaps he is; he tells us—

48

man is but an ass, if he go about to expound this dream.

The ass is "translated" from the third level, where the move is the artisans' and its object is on the first; they must act their absurd play for Theseus. What is its absurdity?—our life, "a tedious brief scene of very tragical mirth," with two lovers suiciding in error, a farcical version of *Romeo and Juliet*. On the fourth level, Oberon is the move and Titania the object; boy must get girl. And, having tidied up the second and third levels, does—he gets Titania, Lysander gets Hermia, Helena gets Demetrius. But the mortals are left in a state of uncertainty:

> Are you sure
> That we are awake? It seems to me
> That yet we sleep, we dream.

In the last act of this tapestry of miraculous textures, the author puts in a word for himself:

THESEUS   The lunatic, the lover, and the poet
　　Are of imagination all compact. . . .
　　And as imagination bodies forth
　　The forms of things unknown, the poet's pen
　　Turns them to shapes, and gives to airy nothing
　　A local habitation and a name. . . .
HIPPOLYTA   But all the story of the night told over,
　　And all their minds transfigured so together,
　　More witnesseth than fancy's images,
　　And grows to something of great constancy.

Several years later, by the guesswork of scholars, the poet was back in the forest in pursuit of gentler game. The opening act of *As You Like It* is a simpler exposi-

49

tion, in three scenes. The first gives us Orlando, hated by his brother, who arranges for the Duke's wrestler to "break his neck" in a match; the behavior of brothers in Shakespeare is dismal. The second scene gives us Rosalind—one of those wit-spiced girls, part boy, who are so delectable in the comedies—losing her heart to Orlando in his victory:

> Sir, you have wrestled well and overthrown
> More than your enemies.

To which Orlando, alone, replies in kind—

> O poor Orlando, thou art overthrown!—

and the lovers' meeting at journey's end is promised; the interest of course lies not in whether it will occur, but how. The "happening" is not yet complete. Rosalind is daughter to the true Duke, already banished by *his* brother, who in the third scene banishes her too—

> Within these ten days if that thou be'st found
> So near our public court as twenty miles,
> Thou diest for it—

and like Hermia's her move is to flee into the forest, disguised for safety as a boy.

Her costume is the entire plot. The moment she discards it in Orlando's view, the play is over; whatever else intervenes, the crowning action must be that encounter between them. She is the move; he, enviable man, is the object.

What happens when move and object fail to meet?— we need look only to the other two levels in this play, each a miscarriage. Orlando's murderous brother on one, the usurping Duke on the other, have substance only in the exposition; as soon as the Duke sends this brother into the woods to look for everybody else the playwright gets bored with them, and these moves never encounter their objects; the brother merely appears in the fourth act with a tale of Orlando saving his life offstage, and of the Duke we hear only that after meeting "an old religious man" he has abdicated. The playwright has cheated us of the promised scenework. The narrative sop he throws us instead won't do, we take it with disgust and disbelief; the very fabric of drama has been liquidated.

So we cling the more to Rosalind's costume, that wisp of structure—but inside it is Rosalind, truer flesh than all the lovers in the complexity of the *Dream*. This play, turning on so flimsy a spring at the center, is almost a mockery of plays—its structure is as cynical as its title —and is in fact more like a walk in the woods; the action meanders through it, an idle creek. Here we are in a genuine forest of

> the uses of adversity;
> Which like the toad, ugly and venomous,
> Wears yet a precious jewel in his head:
> And this our life exempt from public haunt,
> Finds tongues in trees, books in the running brooks,
> Sermons in stones and good in every thing.

Which is to say, it is the artist's inner world. What intervenes between her donning and doffing of costume is Rosalind's testing of Orlando in the "tedious homily of love," a round dance of fools and wenches and Orlando circling Rosalind as a boy, who says—

> Love is merely a madness; and, I tell you, deserves as well a dark house and a whip as madmen do. . . . O coz, coz,

coz, my pretty little coz, that thou didst know how many
fathom deep I am in love!—

but this time all the mistaking is by characters who "fleet
the time carelessly, as they did in the golden world"; and
drifting in and out of the dance is the poet, Jaques,
who asks only

> give me leave
> To speak my mind, and I will through and through
> Cleanse the foul body of the infected world.

In this healing woodland of love and creativity the two
bad brothers no sooner set foot than they are converted;
and in the final scene Rosalind drops her boy's garb,
master move and object meet, the dance is done. All are
restored to the outer world which is the true banishment.
Only the contemplative Jaques remains:

> what you would have
> I'll stay to know at your abandon'd cave.

Tragedy, history, comedy, in all—pick them at random, Iago and Othello, Bolingbroke and Richard II,
Portia and Shylock—the "something of great constancy"
is the master move and object, and their final encounter.
In general, the looser the master move, the more it belongs to comedy; comedy can be a game of chance. In
tragedy it is inexorable, like chess. In both, what is
bridged?—in *Hamlet* an idealistic youth and an old poli-
tician, in *Henry IV* a light rake and a tempestuous man
of war, in *As You Like It* a languishing boy and a playful girl. Opposites. Master move and object are opposites, another datum in the image of man the structure
implies.

This opposition is the eye at the center, without it the playwright cannot see the whole and has no criterion for relevance. Maximally, it is what in *Hamlet* dictates the ghost's first appearance as the "happening," and Hamlet's turn to his tale; forces the playwright—we shall see how —into the chain of great scenes, from exposition to end, which give birth to the unforgettable population of the play; even makes possible the pitch of their utterance, the poetry. Minimally, it promises the integrity of the work.

Is the life of the play in it, then?—of course not, it is the skeleton common to all. Organs, blood, flesh, all that lends each play its individuality is in the intervening matter. Now we must look into where this matter comes from.

8. *The Barrier*

The exposition gives us the master move and object; what hinders their having at each other? If Rosalind promptly offers her love to Orlando, if Hotspur and Prince Hal "chance to meet" outside the tavern and have their duel, if Hamlet at once marches off to stab the King, what have we lost?—the play. The "play," the game. It is what we pay to enjoy; and unless for the next ninety minutes he can hold master move and object apart, the playwright must go back to butchering for his father. He therefore invents a barrier, and its function is contradictory.

It is Rosalind's "doublet and hose" which she uses to keep Orlando near; it is the magic flower which regroups the foursome in reversing pursuit now of Hermia, now of Helena, like a school of fish; it is the war which, rising around Hotspur and Prince Hal, separates them as enemies to be brought together. This barrier is not your everyday fence, it is magnetic, it must draw closer those whom it keeps apart. Does this contradiction sound akin

54

to the bridging of "opposites"?—it is, and in the climactic moment the fence becomes the bridge.

Interposing the barrier makes the play a kind of obstacle course, which the master move must overcome to get at the master object. But such is life. We see the playwright is concerned not only with selling tickets, but with creating an image of our experience; without the barrier, it lacks the sense of life we call truth. Let us follow what happens, then, when a master move is blocked by a barrier.

9. *The Body on the Skeleton*

Of all these plays which crown Renaissance art, so multitudinous of people, embossed by verbal jewelry, antiphonal in subplots and mirror plots, *Othello* is the most direct in its line of action, as spare as a piece of Shaker furniture; every move in it is bred by one man's will. Iago is the man, and the tragic "play" is that of man's will at work in a moral vacuum. It is not primarily about jealousy—unless, of course, it is Iago's.

Iago walks on with Roderigo to begin it, and in the first minute we learn that he serves Othello only

> to serve my turn upon him. . . .
> For when my outward action doth demonstrate
> The native act and figure of my heart
> . . . . 'tis not long after
> But I will wear my heart upon my sleeve
> For daws to peck at: I am not what I am.

The proof is his first move, inciting Roderigo to "plague" Othello "with flies" by rousing Desdemona's father to her elopement. This elopement—or, Othello's love—is the "happening"; it has goaded Iago out of the uneasy equilibrium of his other resentments. In the second scene he is with Othello, all loyalty, when his "flies" descend upon them, Desdemona's father and officers. Othello's move now takes over the middle of the act:

Keep up your bright swords, for the dew will rust them. . . .
Were it my cue to fight, I should have known it
Without a prompter. Where will you that I go
To answer this your charge?

To the Senate chamber, for scene three. Here, amid a military crisis which makes him indispensable, Othello sends for his doting Desdemona, tells the "whole course" of their love in the most famous speech-to-the-jury in literature—

Most potent, grave, and reverend signiors. . . .
That I have ta'en away this old man's daughter,
It is most true—

and wins their blessing; sent to defend Cyprus, he goes off with Desdemona in hand, and leaves the close of the act to Iago. Roderigo for love of the bride threatens to drown himself "incontinently."

IAGO I have looked upon the world for four times seven years; and since I could distinguish betwixt a benefit and an injury, I never found man that knew how to love himself. . . .

RODERIGO I confess it is my shame to be so fond. . . .

IAGO . . . 'tis in ourselves that we are thus or thus. Our bodies are gardens; to the which our wills are gardeners: so that if we will plant nettles or sow lettuce. . . . the power and corrigible authority of this lies in our wills. . . . we have reason to cool . . . our unbitted lusts, whereof I take this, that you call love, to be a sect or scion.

RODERIGO It cannot be.

57

IAGO   It is merely a lust of the blood and a permission of the
will.

Iago's new move is to persuade Roderigo to pursue Desdemona to Cyprus—"Put money in thy purse; follow
thou the wars"—and when alone he targets in on his motive and master move:

> I hate the Moor;
> And it is thought abroad that 'twixt my sheets
> He has done my office:

and now, to get Cassio's place as lieutenant to Othello,
he will "abuse Othello's ear" that Cassio "is too familiar
with *his* wife." But the true root of his malice is what we
see in a cat who plays a chipmunk to death, and walks
away; he is altruistically evil.

So we are given the theme in the play's opposites:
Iago, or solitary will, is—somehow—to undo Othello and
Desdemona, or conjoined love. It is almost a parable, of
our narcissism eating at our capacity to love.

What is the barrier?—Othello's station above Iago, his
eminence and power. But it is precisely this which at-
tracts, he is worthy game. Iago cannot attack frontally,
he must work Othello from within; the barrier is what
draws him closer, it obliges him to become Othello's
intimate.

Thus the exposition. In the following scene, all are
"once more well met at Cyprus"; the war is swept offstage by a storm which, destroying the enemy fleet,
clears the boards for the master move and object; the
working-out begins. Iago, seeing Cassio with Desdemona, says aside—

He takes her by the palm: ay, well said, whisper: with as little a web as this will I ensnare as great a fly as Cassio—

which is one objective, but subordinate; when Othello kisses her, Iago's aside is

> O, you are well tun'd now!
> But I'll set down the pegs that make this music,
> As honest as I am,

which is his other, the master object. His motive as stated concerns us less than the means which still elude him:

> And nothing can or shall content my soul
> Till I am even'd with him, wife for wife;
> Or failing so, yet that I put the Moor
> At least into a jealousy so strong
> That judgement cannot cure. . . .
> I'll have our Michael Cassio on the hip,
> Abuse him to the Moor. . . .
> . . . . 'Tis here, but yet confus'd.

Iago writes this play; from this point on, all its characters act on motives assigned by him, and each is a means to overcome the barrier.

Why then is it not his play?—for a reason we shall come to much later.

First, as Roderigo's intimate, Iago invites him to pick a quarrel with Cassio, and kindles a motive in him by deploring the hanky-panky between Cassio and Desdemona:

IAGO Didst thou not see her paddle with the palm of his hand? didst not mark that?

RODERIGO Yes, that I did; but that was but courtesy.

IAGO Lechery. . . . They met so near with their lips, that their breaths embraced. . . .

59

And Roderigo consents.

Next, in the "night of revels" which marks victory, Iago gets Cassio drunk while on watch, sets Roderigo upon him, and cries up their quarrel into a general brawl which brings Othello out; ordered to testify, Iago is loth but honest—

> I had rather have this tongue cut from my mouth
> Than it should do offense to Michael Cassio;
> Yet—

and damns him in his defense. This step is Iago's next around the barrier; it wins him good marks with Othello—

> I know, Iago,
> Thy honesty and love doth mince this matter,
> Making it light to Cassio—

and it alters two things. Primarily, it separates his two objects, Cassio and Othello, whose judgment is

> Cassio, I love thee;
> But never more be officer of mine.

Secondarily, it makes Iago the intimate now of Cassio; they are left together onstage, and having bred the motive Iago assigns the action.

IAGO   What, are you hurt, lieutenant?

CASSIO   Ay, past all surgery. . . . My reputation, Iago, my reputation!

IAGO   As I am an honest man, I thought you had received some bodily wound. . . . you have lost no reputation at all, unless you repute yourself such a loser. . . . sue to him again. . . .

CASSIO   O God, that men should put an enemy in their

mouths to steal away their brains! . . . I will ask him for
my place again; he shall tell me I am a drunkard! . . . .

IAGO I'll tell you what you shall do. Our general's wife is
now the general. . . . confess yourself freely to her; im-
portune her help to put you in your place again.

And Cassio consents.

Iago, in this step from Roderigo to Cassio, is moving
closer to Othello; he next uses his own wife to effect a
meeting between Cassio and Desdemona, and he leads
Othello to witness its end. They "enter at a distance":

IAGO Ha! I like not that.
OTHELLO What dost thou say?
IAGO Nothing, my lord: or if—I know not what.
OTHELLO Was not that Cassio parted from my wife?
IAGO Cassio, my lord! No, sure, I cannot think it,
   That he would steal away so guilty-like,
   Seeing you coming.

It is Iago's first move that has Othello as face-to-face
object. So opens the crucial quarter-hour scene between
the two—it is defined by the barrier as cunning against
gravitas—which in one long arc will bring Othello to his
knees; we can only skim it, with our eye on Iago and
the barrier, Othello's power. Desdemona begins to plead
Cassio's case, as Iago has arranged:

DESDEMONA   Good love, call him back.
OTHELLO Not now, sweet Desdemona; some other time.
DESDEMONA But shall 't be shortly?
OTHELLO   The sooner, sweet, for you. . . .
DESDEMONA Tomorrow dinner, then?
OTHELLO   I shall not dine at home;
   I meet the captains at the citadel.
DESDEMONA Why, then tomorrow night; or Tuesday morn;

On Tuesday noon, or night; on Wednesday morn:
I prithee name the time. . . .

Othello puts her off, and she leaves; now Iago moves in.

OTHELLO   Excellent wretch! Perdition catch my soul,
But I do love thee! and when I love thee not,
Chaos is come again.
IAGO   My noble lord,—
OTHELLO   What dost thou say, Iago?
IAGO   Did Michael Cassio, when you woo'd my lady,
Know of your love?
OTHELLO   He did, from first to last: why dost thou ask?
IAGO   But for a satisfaction of my thought;
No further harm.
OTHELLO   Why of thy thought, Iago?
IAGO   I did not think he had been acquainted with her.
OTHELLO   O, yes, and went between us very oft.
IAGO   Indeed!
OTHELLO   Indeed! ay, indeed: discern'st thou aught in that?
Is he not honest?
IAGO   Honest, my lord!
OTHELLO   Honest! ay, honest.
IAGO   My lord, for aught I know.
OTHELLO   What dost thou think?
IAGO   Think, my lord!
OTHELLO   Think, my lord! By heaven, he echoes me,
As if there were some monster in his thought
Too hideous to be shown. . . . If thou dost love me,
Show me thy thought.

Given his motive by Iago, Othello is now on the move,
and Iago as object refuses him:

IAGO   I am not bound to that all slaves are free to.
Utter my thoughts? Why, say that they are vile and
false. . . .
OTHELLO   Thou dost conspire against thy friend, Iago,

If thou but think'st him wrong'd and mak'st his ear
A stranger to thy thoughts. . . .
IAGO   It were not for your quiet nor your good. . . .
Good name in man and woman, dear my lord,
Is the immediate jewel of their souls:
Who steals my purse steals trash—

It is not what he has told Cassio, and it does not impress
Othello; in Iago's script, his eminence must "overbear"
Iago.

OTHELLO   By heaven, I'll know thy thoughts. . . .
IAGO   O, beware, my lord, of jealousy;
It is the green-eyed monster which doth mock
The meat it feeds on. . . .
OTHELLO   Think'st thou I'ld make a life of jealousy,
To follow still the changes of the moon
With fresh suspicions? . . . . No, Iago,
I'll see before I doubt; when I doubt, prove;
And, on the proof, there is no more but this,
Away at once with love or jealousy!
IAGO   I am glad of it; for now I shall have reason
To show the love and duty that I bear you
With franker spirit. . . . I speak not yet of proof.
Look to your wife. . . .

So Iago reacquires the move he has never relinquished,
and like an angler works the hook deeper into Othello,
letting out line and drawing it in:

IAGO   She did deceive her father, marrying you;
And when she seem'd to shake and fear your looks,
She loved them most.
OTHELLO   And so she did. . . .
IAGO   I see this hath a little dash'd your spirits.
OTHELLO   Not a jot, not a jot. . . .
IAGO   I am to pray you not to strain my speech

> To grosser issues nor to larger reach
> Than to suspicion.
> OTHELLO   I will not. . . .
> IAGO My lord, I see you're moved.
> OTHELLO   No, not much moved;
>   I do not think but Desdemona's honest.
> IAGO Long live she so! and long live you to think so!
> OTHELLO And yet, how nature erring from itself—
> IAGO Ay, there's the point. . . .

Desdemona, re-entering, drops her handkerchief; it is the one "accident" in the play, Iago's wife delivers it to him, and he immediately weaves it into the web—he will "lose" it in Cassio's room. This brief interruption serves a further function, it suggests an unbrief passage of time while Othello simmers. The move is—seemingly—his, and when he returns to the scene his doubts boil over to scald Iago:

> OTHELLO Villain, be sure thou prove my love a whore,
>   Be sure of it; give me the ocular proof;
>   Or, by the worth of mine eternal soul,
>   Thou hadst been better have been born a dog
>   Than answer my waked wrath!
> IAGO   Is't come to this?
> OTHELLO Make me to see't. . . . or woe upon thy life!

Iago "repents" his honesty, and starts out—his second refusal, which makes Othello repent his wrath; but he must have evidence, and Iago supplies two bits.

> IAGO I lay with Cassio lately. . . .
>   In sleep I heard him say, 'Sweet Desdemona,
>   Let us be wary, let us hide our loves;'
>   . . . . then kiss me hard,
>   As if he pluck'd up kisses by the roots,

That grew upon my lips: then laid his leg
Over my thigh, and sigh'd, and kiss'd. . . .
OTHELLO   O monstrous! . . . .
IAGO   She may be honest yet. Tell me but this;
Have you not sometimes seen a handkerchief
Spotted with strawberries in your wife's hand?
OTHELLO   I gave her such a one; 'twas my first gift.
IAGO   . . . . such a handkerchief—
I am sure it was your wife's—did I today
See Cassio wipe his beard with.

Othello in a rage falls to his knees to swear "black ven-
geance," and Iago joins him:

OTHELLO   Now, by yond marble heaven,
In the due reverence of a sacred vow
I here engage my words.
IAGO   Do not rise yet.
Witness, you ever-burning lights above . . .
Witness that here Iago doth give up
The execution of his wit, hands, heart,
To wrong'd Othello's service! . . . .
OTHELLO   . . . Now art thou my lieutenant.
IAGO   I am your own for ever.

The barrier still exists; but Iago is now inside it.

It has taken him nine moves in as many scenes to win
Cassio's place, and come within reach of his master object; and only after two more acts will he bring these
lovers to their deathbed. In keeping the master move and
object apart, the barrier has forced Iago to outwit it, that
is, to think out a sequence of steps around it. If this play
is an organism, Iago is surely its brain, but why?—because the barrier forces him into the intellection of intrigue. Or, plays midwife to his character.

Character?—we are, suddenly, no longer in the realm

of structural mechanics; our thumb is on the living pulse of a person, the why and what and how of him. Where did this happen? In the scenework, and we begin to see that scenework and character are two aspects of one process.

In each step around the barrier, Iago not only commits to visible action the "native figure" of his soul, and so comes to "be" for us, an objectified reality; he compels the other characters in turn—Desedemona's father, Othello, Roderigo, Cassio—likewise to act and "be." Thus, his inviting Roderigo into the needed quarrel is a scene, as defined: Iago has the move, Roderigo is the object, and one must be altered. The what-and-how of the move is Iago, and the scene has been obligated by the barrier as his next step around it. If Roderigo consents he is one kind of man, and if he refuses, another; either way, the barrier has forced the scene which forces now the characterization of Roderigo, or the what and the how of him. It is the opposition of the what-and-how of the two characters which makes up the dramatic substance of the scene, will against will. Likewise with Iago's awakening of Othello's doubts; it is a scene, with Iago on the move and Othello the object, and one must be altered. It has been obligated by the barrier, and step by step the opposition of the what-and-how of the two characters makes up its dramatic substance, will against will. Both scenes, and every other, come about as maneuvers around the barrier.

It is precisely here that we pass from the skeleton to the body of the play. From its first minute to that at which we broke off, the theatrical meat of it—Desdemona's father rushing in with torches to arrest Othello, and Othello's majestic defense before the Senate, and Iago coaxing Roderigo's gleam of lust into service as his "purse," and Cassio in the drunken brawl which has the stage in an uproar, and Desdemona prettily pleading for him with Othello, and Othello writhing on the hook which works him into a murderous rage—all that we later remember as the true life of the piece is born here; we are at the source of the "intervening matter."

What happens then when a master move is blocked by a barrier?—everything. The body of a play, we said, is a working-out of the intervening matter; and now we see how such matter gets into the play. The riches of character, each confrontation and fresh decision, the very speech which effects it—other terms for what I have called move, object, alteration—all these come into existence only because the barrier stands between the master move and object. It is the effort to get through the barrier that breeds the intervening matter, and crystallizes in the chain of scenes.

Deeper than this we cannot fruitfully dig; the depths in himself which this playwright draws upon to flesh out the scenework lie beyond the edge of our scrutiny, they are the mystery of his creative gift.

10. *Aside*

And yet—

If I stand at the rim of the Grand Canyon I see a staggering disorder of rock peaks by the hundreds; somewhere among them is a river, but unseen, and the chaos of buttes, mesas, voids, is simply unintelligible. If I hike down and across, from rim to rim, the structure is clear. A mile below is the river which has gouged the basic canyon from east to west; my way down to it follows a creek, which has gouged a side canyon from south to north; in this secondary canyon I pass other canyons gouged from every direction, but all creekwards, and if I go up one of these tertiary canyons I come upon still others, tributary to it. The chaos of peaks is sculptured by this maze of countless stream-beds, all headed for the river below. Since one principle is at work in all—the move of water ruining rock—it is not surprising that a gully at the top, the mile-deep riverbed at the bottom, and all the subsidiary canyons between, share the same structure; it reproduces itself on level after level.

So with the immense structures of these plays; one principle is at work on level after level, the move of human will against barriers.

Let us fill in our definition of the scene; in it we find a barrier too. Thus, when Hamlet confronts the ghost the barrier his move must overcome is the ghost's silence before others, and when Isabella confronts Angelo the barrier her move must overcome is his blindness to all but the law. To the earlier question, Is the play, like the scene, definable in terms of the move? the answer is yes, of course. It is a super-scene, in which the master move overcomes the barrier to find the master object; and this encounter is arrived at by means of the scenework itself—in which, conversely, each scene is a miniature play with a barrier of its own. The sum total of the moves which dissolve the barriers in the scenes is born of, and gives birth to, the master move which dissolves the barrier to the master object. From the first move on, the structures of the work thus reproduce each other on successive levels, and the organic intricacy of the form has its own beauty.

But a form is to contain; what is contained in this one? The first move against the first barrier en route to the first object implies an opposing, or contradiction. But in the chain of scenes, we saw that what is object in one is quickened into move in the next, a doubling of contradictory flux. To it, we added the contradictory charge of opposites in master move and object. To them, we added the contradictory work of the barrier in drawing them closer to be kept apart, and suggested a further contradiction, the barrier will be the bridge between them. If the inner stresses of the play are so unrelievedly contradictory, it helps explain the rigor and unity of the form needed to contain them.

Is it too much to say that in examining drama as a form we are in the playpen of contradiction itself, that is, willy-nilly are contemplating its nature as a dialectic in the mind?—which cannot be irrelevant to the mystery of the creative gift.

II. *The Third-Act Pivot*

We find ourselves now in the middle of the working-out, and have defined it in all but words. It is the sequence of twists and turns the master move is compelled to take around the barrier in getting at the master object; and it includes the twists and turns the master object is compelled to take in defending itself. Both, in the process, exact twists and turns from the subordinate personae around them. And out of this welter of moves and countermoves arises the body of the play, those attributes—its events and characters, their language, the mood, the tempo, the comic or tragic "meaning"—which we experience as its unique identity.

These plays are read now as five-act structures. It is not necessarily how the playwright saw them; no division into acts or scenes was made in the quartos published during his lifetime, and in the posthumous collection of 1623 the division is fitful—complete in *The Tempest*, fragmentary for two acts in *Hamlet* and missing thereafter, not even begun in *Romeo and Juliet*.

Much of the act-and-scene numbering is the work of editors a century later. Not foolish, it defines organic chunks in the writing of these and all plays. In those of subsequent centuries—for reasons I won't explore here, ranging from technical inventions in scenery and lighting to social shifts in audience and content—we see the number of acts shrink, to four, then three, and most recently two; in all, the business of the working-out remains the same, only its distribution changes. In the five-act structure, then, the close of the third act brings us to a most pregnant moment, when structure articulates theme.

In *Othello* we have followed the working-out to the penultimate scene of the third act, where Othello charges Iago to tell him within three days "that Cassio's not alive," and talks wildly also of "death for the fair devil"; its closing scene turns on the handkerchief. When Desdemona again presses her suit for Cassio, Othello demands the handkerchief—

DESDEMONA   This is a trick to put me from my suit:
   Pray you, let Cassio be received again.
OTHELLO   Fetch me the handkerchief; my mind misgives.
DESDEMONA   Come, come;
   You'll never meet a more sufficient man.
OTHELLO   The handkerchief!
DESDEMONA   I pray, talk me of Cassio.
OTHELLO   The handkerchief!
DESDEMONA   A man that all his time
   Hath founded his good fortunes on your love,
   Shared dangers with you,—
OTHELLO   The handkerchief!
DESDEMONA   In sooth, you are to blame.
OTHELLO   Away!—

72

and leaves her in a rage; we then see Cassio with the handkerchief in hand.

Here the third act ends. In it Iago has not only become Othello's confidant, he has effected the first overt breach between the lovers, and has in Cassio's hand the means to undo them totally; the third act has lifted us to a turning-point in this war between solitary will and conjoined love. The action now, in the last third, will plunge on to the final disaster. Is this turning-point in the course of the working-out fortuitous in this play?—no, we find it in every third act, tragedy, history, or comedy, and the working-out is aimed at it from the start.

So in *Macbeth* it is the third-act pivot which gives us the murder of Banquo and his hallucinatory reappearance as ghost at the feast, undoing Macbeth—

> It will have blood; they say blood will have blood:
> Stones have been known to move and trees to speak;
> Augures and understood relations have
> By maggot-pies and choughs and rooks brought forth
> The secret'st man of blood—

and ends with news of Macduff raising armies in England; the play has turned for its plunge.

In *Richard II* it is the third-act pivot which gives us Richard back from Ireland, to the melting away of his supporters and his first meeting with a victorious Bolingbroke since banishing him—

RICHARD What says King Bolingbroke? will his majesty
  Give Richard leave to live till Richard die?
  You make a leg, and Bolingbroke says ay.
NORTHUMBERLAND My lord, in the base court he doth attend

To speak with you; may it please you to come down.
RICHARD Down, down I come; like glistering Phaeton,
Wanting the manage of unruly jades.
In the base court? Base court, where kings grow base,
To come at traitors' calls and do them grace.
In the base court? Come down? Down, court! Down,
king!

and down he comes, in his descent to abdication and
death; at the act's end two gardeners serve as Greek
chorus.

SERVANT Why should we in the compass of a pale
Keep law and form and due proportion,
Showing, as in a model, our firm estate,
When our sea-walled garden, the whole land,
Is full of weeds; her fairest flowers choked up,
Her fruit-trees all unpruned, her hedges ruin'd,
Her knots disorder'd, and her wholesome herbs
Swarming with caterpillars?
GARDENER   Hold thy peace:
He that hath suffer'd this disorder'd spring
Hath now himself met with the fall of leaf. . . .
. . . Oh, what pity is it,
That he had not so trimm'd and dress'd his land,
As we this garden!

In *The Taming of the Shrew* it is the third-act pivot
which gives us the "mad marriage" of Katharina and
Petruchio in his rags, swearing at the altar and kissing
the bride's lips "with such a clamorous smack that at the
parting all the church did echo," and in the teeth of her
refusal to depart with him Petruchio's credo as theme—

I will be master of what is mine own:
She is my goods, my chattels; she is my house,

74

My household stuff, my field, my barn,
My horse, my ox, my ass, my any thing,

and he carries her off with sword drawn against the world and women's lib.

In *Julius Caesar* it is the third-act pivot which gives us his assassination and the tour-de-force of Antony's funeral speech, turning the citizenry—that collective character, "you blocks, you stones, you worse than senseless things" of the play's first scene—into a riotous mob that tears to pieces Cinna the poet:

ANTONY   Now let it work. Mischief, thou art afoot,
Take thou what course thou wilt—

and the death-struggle for state power is on.

And in *Coriolanus* it is the third-act pivot which brings that hero, not unlike a poet himself in the hands of the rabble, to the crossroads of his life: mainstay of a state whose populace he cannot abide, elected to high honor for his exploits and in the same hour stripped of it for his contempt, he is banished from Rome forever, denounces his critics—

You common cry of curs! whose breath I hate
As reek o' the rotten fens, whose loves I prize
As the dead carcasses of unburied men
That do corrupt my air, I banish you. . . .
There is a world elsewhere—

and leaves to die at its hands.

This pivot at the heart of the work, always expressive of the theme, provides us with a convenient overlook in the working-out of complicated plots. In the tragedies the plot inclines to be monophonic; the comedies, made up of weaker actions which buttress each other, incline to double or triple plotting. Here let us look into the first two-thirds of two specimens, a comedy and a tragedy, both double-plotted.

12. *Double Plot, Comic*

In *The Merchant of Venice* we are given two stories, and each has its own working-out. The first concerns Portia's three caskets and is one of "chance" events, external to and unaffected by the will of any of its characters; thus it is narrative, and of itself would not suffice to hold the stage. It is however stitched at several points to the second, which in Shylock and the pound of flesh gives us the willing of true drama, and carries the first. They rise in parallel motion from the exposition to the third-act pivot.

The first stitch, after some badinage, is what opens the play—

ANTONIO   Well, tell me now, what lady is the same
   To whom you swore a secret pilgrimage,
   That you today promised to tell me of? . . . .
BASSANIO   In Belmont is a lady richly left;
   And she is fair, and, fairer than that word,
   Of wondrous virtues. . . .
   Nor is the wide world ignorant of her worth;
   For the four winds blow in from every coast
   Renowned suitors. . . .

> O my Antonio, had I but the means
> To hold a rival place with one of them. . . .
> ANTONIO   Thou know'st that all my fortunes are at sea;
>   Neither have I money, nor commodity
>   To raise a present sum: therefore go forth;
>   Try what my credit can in Venice do—

and with this as the "happening" both stories grow from a single action. In the second scene we pick up Portia sighing in Belmont—

> By my troth, Nerissa, my little body is aweary of this great world. . . . I may neither choose whom I would, nor refuse whom I dislike; so is the will of a living daughter curbed by the will of a dead father,

an eccentric gentleman who has bequeathed her and his estate to a lottery, three caskets of gold, silver, and lead; she must wed the suitor who chooses right. Of all who beset her she takes a dim view:

> I had rather be married to a death's-head with a bone in his mouth. . . .

She is a saucy girl, with sufficient will, but there is no room to exercise it in Belmont; "curbed" by the premise, she is merely awaiting her fate, and the scene—it is not a true scene, but a story-point—closes on news of still another suitor. A story-point I define as a turn of information or event that enters the action from outside, by the author's fiat. With the third scene we are back to drama; it gives us Shylock as object, and the move is again Bassanio's.

> BASSANIO   May you stead me? will you pleasure me? shall I know your answer?

SHYLOCK   Three thousand ducats for three months, and Antonio bound.
BASSANIO   Your answer to that. . . .
SHYLOCK   I will bethink me. May I speak with Antonio?
BASSANIO   If it please you to dine with us.
SHYLOCK   Yes, to smell pork; to eat of the habitation which
your prophet the Nazarite conjured the devil into. I will
buy with you, sell with you, talk with you, walk with
you, and so following; but I will not eat with you, drink
with you, nor pray with you.

So the "opposites" of this story are invoked at once,
Christian and Jew, but the playwright is stalking a larger
beast than anti-Semitism. Enter Antonio, who now takes
on Bassanio's move as his own; it cuts Bassanio loose for
the other story.

ANTONIO   Shylock, although I neither lend nor borrow,
   By taking nor by giving of excess,
   Yet, to supply the ripe wants of my friend,
   I'll break a custom. Is he yet possess'd
   How much ye would?
SHYLOCK   Ay, ay, three thousand ducats. . . .
ANTONIO   Well, Shylock, shall we be beholding to you?

The move has passed to Shylock, and he acquaints us—
note, it is give-and-take, drama—with the tensions which
antecede the happening:

SHYLOCK   Signior Antonio, many a time and oft
   In the Rialto you have rated me
   About my moneys and my usances:
   Still have I borne it with a patient shrug;
   For sufferance is the badge of all our tribe.
   You call me misbeliever, cut-throat dog,
   And spit upon my Jewish gaberdine,
   And all for use of that which is mine own.

79

Well then, it now appears you need my help:
Go to, then; you come to me, and you say
'Shylock, we would have moneys:' you say so;
You, that did void your rheum upon my beard,
And foot me as you spurn a stranger cur
Over your threshold: moneys is your suit.
What should I say to you? . . . .
'Fair sir, you spit on me on Wednesday last;
You spurn'd me such a day; another time
You call'd me dog; and for these courtesies
I'll lend you thus much moneys'?

ANTONIO   I am as like to call thee so again,
To spit on thee again, to spurn thee too.
If thou wilt lend this money, lend it not
As to thy friends. . . .
But lend it rather to thine enemy;
Who if he break, thou mayst with better face
Exact the penalty.

SHYLOCK   Why, look you, how you storm!
I would be friends with you. . . .
Supply your present wants, and take no doit
Of usance for my moneys. . . .

BASSANIO   This were kindness.

SHYLOCK   This kindness will I show.
Go with me to a notary, seal me there
Your single bond; and, in a merry sport,
If you repay me not on such a day, . . .
Be nominated for an equal pound
Of your fair flesh, to be cut off and taken
In what part of your body pleaseth me.

It is Antonio's move, and over Bassanio's objection he accepts the "merry sport."

The exposition, simple and clean, is complete with the first act: it has established the antagonists in the story which is drama, and the lovers in the story which is narrative. Seemingly—but again the structure guards a thematic secret—the spring at the center is double. We are promised two decisive encounters, one between Antonio and Shylock, the other between Bassanio and Portia; the barrier for Antonio is the legal compulsion of the bond, the barrier for Bassanio is the riddle of the caskets. No connection is promised, we know only that the unity of drama requires it. Although we must expect the narrative by its nature to be low in scenework, both stories now undergo a working-out, and each is aimed at the third-act pivot.

They develop alternately. The second act opens in Belmont, as the Prince of Morocco reports to choose a casket, and the actual choice is deferred to keep us curious. Back in Venice, we have a chain of scenelets, all bustle, in which Bassanio picks up companions for his voyage to Belmont and sets sail; the most notable among them is Shylock's daughter, eloping, with her father's ducats. It is another stitch between the two stories, and that of the bond is kept alive midway in the bustle by a vivid sketch of Shylock at home, fussing over how much his servant eats and denouncing the music which adorns the alternate love story:

> What, are there masques? Hear you me, Jessica:
> Lock up my doors; and when you hear the drum,
> And the vile squealing of the wry-neck'd fife,
> Clamber not you up to the casements then,
> Nor thrust your head into the public street
> To gaze on Christian fools with varnish'd faces;
> But stop my house's ears, I mean my casements:
> Let not the sound of shallow foppery enter
> My sober house.

In Belmont again, Morocco chooses the gold casket, and finds in it a skull with a scroll in its eyehole, "All that glisters is not gold"—Portia thinks it "a gentle riddance"; it echoes Shylock. Back in Venice, we learn from street gossip that he is running about crying for his daughter and his ducats, and the playwright adds another stitch:

> Let good Antonio look he keep his day,
> Or he shall pay for this.

In Belmont again, the Prince of Arragon chooses the silver casket, to find in it "the portrait of a blinking idiot," another echo of money, and a servant announces Bassanio's arrival to an eager Portia. This is all skipping stuff, an act of story-points, nine scenelets of narrative bits and pieces held in a dramatic suspension only by the bizarre threat of Shylock's bond; but they carry us into the third act, terra firma.

It opens with another scrap of street gossip, Antonio has a ship wrecked, and now—we see that all the irrelevance of the elopement was preparation for it—Shylock's move takes over the act:

SHYLOCK You knew, none so well, none so well as you, of my daughter's flight.

SALARINO That's certain: I, for my part, knew the tailor that made the wings she flew withal. . . .

SHYLOCK My own flesh and blood to rebel! . . . .

SALARINO But tell us, do you hear whether Antonio have had any loss at sea or no? . . . .

SHYLOCK Let him look to his bond: he was wont to call me usurer; let him look to his bond. . . .

SALARINO Why, I am sure, if he forfeit, thou will not take his flesh: what's that good for?

SHYLOCK To bait fish withal: if it will feed nothing else,

it will feed my revenge. . . . I am a Jew. Hath not a Jew eyes? hath not a Jew hands, organs, dimensions, senses, affections, passions? fed with the same food, hurt with the same weapons, subject to the same diseases, healed by the same means, warmed and cooled by the same winter and summer, as a Christian is? If you prick us, do we not bleed? if you tickle us, do we not laugh? if you poison us, do we not die? and if you wrong us, shall we not revenge? . . . . I will have the heart of him, if he forfeit. . . .

It is a famous statement of the universality of man, but still not the larger beast the playwright is after. The second scene whisks us back to Belmont, where the lovers are met at last:

> PORTIA   I pray you, tarry: pause a day or two
>   Before you hazard. . . . Beshrew your eyes,
>   They have o'er-look'd me, and divided me;
>   One half of me is yours, the other half yours,
>   Mine own, I would say; but if mine, then yours,
>   And so all yours! . . .
> BASSANIO   Let me choose;
>   For as I am, I live upon the rack.

No surprise, he chooses the lead casket, and finds in it Portia's picture. A love lyric, this choice is written—with music under—at twice the length of the earlier two, and so culminates the *flow* of the half which is narrative; the *pounce* of the drama is upon it at once, in a letter delivered.

> BASSANIO   O sweet Portia,
>   Here are a few of the unpleasant'st words
>   That ever blotted paper!

It comes from Antonio:

'Sweet Bassanio, my ships have all miscarried, my creditors grow cruel, my estate is very low, my bond to the Jew is forfeit; and since in paying it, it is impossible I should live, all debts are cleared between you and I, if I might but see you at my death.'

Bassanio turns back to Venice, his move. It promises nothing, and the third scene gives us Antonio's, equally ineffectual; in the hands of a gaoler, he pleads with Shylock.

SHYLOCK   Gaoler, look to him: tell not me of mercy. . . .
ANTONIO   Hear me yet, good Shylock.
SHYLOCK   I'll have my bond; speak not against my bond:
   I have sworn an oath that I will have my bond.
   Thou call'dst me dog before thou hadst a cause;
   But, since I am a dog, beware my fangs:
   The Duke shall grant me justice. . . .
ANTONIO   I pray thee, hear me speak.
SHYLOCK   I'll have my bond; I will not hear thee speak:
   I'll have my bond. . . . Follow not;
   I'll have no speaking. . . .
ANTONIO   I'll follow him no more with bootless prayers.
   . . . . Pray God, Bassanio come
   To see me pay his debt, and then I care not!

Who has the next move?—none of them, the play is dead-locked. But now we are at its turning-point, the scene which illuminates the entire structure. Portia puts the "manage of my house" into other hands, sends a messenger off for legal opinion and garments, and leaves for Venice with her waiting-maid, "accoutred like young men."

   NERISSA   Why, shall we turn to men?
   PORTIA   Fie, what a question's that,
      If thou wert near a lewd interpreter!

> But come, I'll tell thee all my whole device
> When I am in my coach, which stays for us
> At the park-gate.

She is off of course to play lawyer in Antonio's cause; at precisely the third-act pivot the two stories have become one.

And it is only in their union that the structure, and the theme implicit in it, rise to unmistakable view. Is the play anti-Semitic?—undeniably, for however in these acts the playwright is at pains to "justify" Shylock as victim, he etches him with too many odious touches to be let off the charge. But the portrait, so violent that it dominates the play, is the labor of a loving hand; and the joys of love's labor are not irrelevant. For with the third-act pivot we see that it is, more than the characters, the two stories themselves which are the opposites of the play. Shylock's is as steeped in gloom and hate—the word is common in his mouth—as Portia's is in joy and love; and in the trial scene which follows, his eye-for-an-eye morality—

> What judgement shall I dread, doing no wrong?
> . . . . I stand here for law—

is capped by her great plea for the mercy which

> droppeth as the gentle rain from heaven. . . .
> It is an attribute to God himself;
> And earthly power doth then show likest God's
> When mercy seasons justice.

The larger beast caught in the net of this structure is the shift from the masculine ethic of the Old Testament to the feminine ethic of the New; and a woman is the advocate.

So much for Petruchio.

This play is comedy, in which chance allows a loose-ness of scenework; hyperbolically speaking, there is but one scene in the play, the trial, and the casket narrative in these acts may be viewed as a bringing up of the artillery for it, a three-act exposition. For a more remorseless working-out of a double plot we must turn to tragedy.

13. *Surrogates*

First, a parenthesis.

From his entrance in this comedy Shylock as antagonist stands in it like a pillar. But for three acts he has no opposite; how does the playwright manipulate the movement? By a piece of prestidigitation.

Bassanio has the first move, in soliciting the loan, and is thus the earliest candidate for the role of other antagonist; but he is needed in Belmont for the love story. Antonio supplants him—"Shall *we* be beholding to you?" —and now we seem to have a genuine opposite. Not so, it is only a holding action. But it is strong enough to keep us watching for another two acts; and not until the third-act pivot when Portia in turn supplants Antonio do we have the true antagonists exposed. We have been led on by surrogates, like Angelo's old flame in the dark of his bed.

The brief assumption of one character's function by another is not uncommon—when Lucio aside urges Isabella on, "Kneel down before him, hang upon his gown," he is speaking as her brother's surrogate—but

here we see it used as major architecture. It is a varia-
tion-form of the structure we have been studying; one
of the two antagonists may become a committee.

So in the "history" of *Richard III*. In this chronicle the
protagonist acquaints us with his object in an opening
soliloquy:

> Deform'd, unfinish'd, sent before my time
> Into this breathing world, scarce half made up,
> And that so lamely and unfashionable
> That dogs bark at me. . . .
> I am determined to prove a villain,

revenge himself on the world, and—as it transpires—wear
a crown. The barrier to it consists of most of the other
characters, and he strews his path to it with their corpses.
In the third-act pivot he "consents" to be crowned; the
question then is

> But shall we wear these honours for a day?
> Or shall they last, and we rejoice in them?

and his answer is more murders. It is a somewhat tedious
career—and the more so for us because of inadequate exposition, the playwright assumes we already know the
history of that court's in-fighting, as his audience did—
but it is enlivened by the zest for evil of "that bottled
spider, that poisonous bunch-back'd toad," who carries
on until the battle of Salisbury in the fifth act; there he
is slain by a virtuous adversary, Richmond, whom we
have not hitherto met. Where in this structure is the
other antagonist?—that committee of corpses who prepared us for Richmond, serving as his surrogates.

Footnote, this virtuous adversary will found the Tu-
dor dynasty—under which our playwright lived—and it

is his royal version which "became" history; subsequent studies suggest that Richard III was a gentle liberal who was beloved of all, murdered no one, and had no hunchback.

So too in the tragedy of *Macbeth*, whose object is identical, to seize the crown and wear it in good health. He is "enkindled" unto this by the witches—"All hail, Macbeth! that shalt be king hereafter"—and in his course he hurdles five acts of barriers. In the first act it is his own dread, which his Lady helps prod him over; it will recur. In the second act it is King Duncan, whom he murders in his sleep, together with his guards who are to bear the blame; and we are given Macduff—no johnny-come-lately like Richmond—who discovers the body and swears, with Banquo, to fight "treasonous malice." In the third act it is Banquo; Macbeth remembers that the witches

> hail'd him father to a line of kings:
> Upon my head they placed a fruitless crown. . . .
> For Banquo's issue have I filed my mind;
> For them the gracious Duncan have I murder'd—

and he sets murderers upon him and his son; the son escapes, and the dread returns as Banquo's ghost at the feast, which Macduff boycotts—he is fled to raise armies. In the fourth act it is Macduff's wife and children, slaughtered by the murderers in his stead. In the fifth act it is young Siward, of the avenging armies, whom Macbeth kills in combat; enter Macduff, and kills Macbeth. Introduced early enough and recurrent throughout, Macduff is a seeming antagonist, but too pale a one to counterpoise Macbeth; he is but an agent. The true antagonist is characterological fate personified by a gaggle of witches, which Macbeth cannot hurdle, and all the others are surrogates.

These plays are dominated by a figure so compelling that he carries the whole on his own back, surrogates and all; each of the three has become an archetype. Given a character of sufficient force, it is possible to fracture any rule of playmaking, except one. It is not possible to have surrogates for such a character also; look at any of the plays which have failed to hold the stage.

Now let us turn to a tragedy which has, in addition to a double plot, another character of legendary size.

14. *Double Plot, Tragic*

The two stories in *King Lear* are not opposites; they are the same story, in two versions. Lear has three daughters, Gloucester two sons; both are betrayed by the bad children to whom they are so good, and rescued by the good to whom they are so bad; each old man undergoes an extreme of suffering, and dies of a broken heart. Why this mirroring?—structurally it is the enigma of the play. The Lear version is based on an earlier "comedy," the Gloucester version on the tale of another king; it is our playwright who has braided them into one work, the most hopeless of his tragedies. So deliberate a braiding cannot be needless, but to resolve the enigma we must follow each version through the second act.

The exposition of Lear's occurs entirely in the opening scene, which we first examined in defining the move. Lear resolves to divide his kingdom, the "happening"; and its immediate consequences are that he disinherits Cordelia, exiles Kent, and endows Regan and Goneril with the whole. Let us defer for a bit the question here of the antagonists and the barrier.

The first-page chat which prefaces this exposition has already begun the other—

KENT   Is not this your son, my lord?

GLOUCESTER   His breeding, sir, hath been at my charge: I have so often blushed to acknowledge him that now I am brazed to it.

KENT   I cannot conceive you.

GLOUCESTER   Sir, this young fellow's mother could: whereupon she grew round-wombed, and had, indeed, sir, a son for her cradle ere she had a husband for her bed. . . .

KENT   I must love you, and sue to know you better.

EDMUND   Sir, I shall study deserving—

and the second scene completes it. Edmund resolves to dispossess his half-brother Edgar, the "happening" here; that is, he will wrest from Gloucester by his own move that which Regan and Goneril have been granted by Lear's. He baits Gloucester into reading a forged letter—

GLOUCESTER   '. . . . If our father would sleep till I waked him, you should enjoy half his revenue for ever, and live the beloved of your brother, Edgar'. . . . Abominable villain! Where is he?

EDMUND   I do not well know, my lord. If it shall please you to suspend your indignation against my brother till you can derive from him better testimony of his intent, you should run a certain course—

and promises a meeting "where you shall hear us confer of this." Gloucester attributes the treachery to "these late eclipses in the sun and moon"; Edmund when alone thinks this

the excellent foppery of the world, that when we are sick in fortune—often the surfeit of our own behavior—we make guilty of our disasters the sun, the moon and the stars: as if

we were villains by necessity. . . . drunkards, liars, and
adulterers, by an enforced obedience of planetary influence.

He believes rather in human will, and without delay he
exercises his by informing Edgar their father is so enraged at him that

> . . . . with the mischief of your person it would scarcely
> allay.
>
> EDGAR   Some villain hath done me wrong.
> EDMUND   That's my fear. . . . If you do stir abroad, go
> armed.
> EDGAR   Armed, brother!
> EDMUND   Brother, I advise you to the best: go armed: I am
> no honest man if there be any good meaning towards
> you—

and bids him hide till Gloucester's "rage goes slower."
Edmund tags the scene with a promise, to himself and us:

> I see the business.
> Let me, if not by birth, have lands by wit:
> All with me's meet that I can fashion fit.

There is little "past" in the play—it endangers the
premise, more memory of their relatives and these old
men would be less nitwitty about them—and we are now
done with exposition; the working-out begins in the initial act. It will proceed in alternate chunks, as in *The
Merchant of Venice*, but this time not by story-points.
Story-points, as capricious events entering from outside,
are destructive of tragedy, whose inevitability must be
self-evident; we find it so only when the events arise inexorably from the give-and-take of scenework. In this
play the scenes are much counterpointed with other matter, and dwarf those we looked at earlier.

93

The first chunk comprises three scenes which in truth are one. It opens on Goneril in her palace; Lear has struck one of her servants, which exasperates her:

> By day and night he wrongs me; every hour
> He flashes into one gross crime or other,
> That sets us all at odds. I'll not endure it.

It is her move, with Lear as the object, and she will make it in two steps; first, she tells her steward to

> come slack of former services. . . .

OSWALD   He's coming, madam; I hear him.

GONERIL   Put on what weary negligence you please,
You and your fellows; I'd have it come to question:
If he distaste it, let him to my sister.

The promise is set, and permits a parenthesis. Into the hall steals Kent, disguised, for his own move. Lear comes in, no less royal than hitherto—"Let me not stay a jot for dinner; go get it ready"—and in a mini-scene Kent asks to serve him.

LEAR   Dost thou know me, fellow?

KENT   No, sir; but you have that in your countenance which I would fain call master.

LEAR   What's that?

KENT   Authority.

LEAR   . . . . thou shalt serve me: if I like thee no worse after dinner, I will not part from thee yet.

Now comes Oswald's turn to deliver the first half of Goneril's move; he slights Lear, and in response is struck by the King, tripped by Kent, and kicked out. It has "come to question," and we await Goneril's second step.

So another parenthesis may enter:

94

FOOL Let me hire him too: here's my coxcomb. . . .

KENT Why, Fool?

FOOL Why, for taking one's part that's out of favour. . . .
Would I had two coxcombs and two daughters!

LEAR Why, my boy?

FOOL · If I gave them all my living, I'ld keep my coxcombs
myself. There's mine; beg another of thy daughters. . . .

LEAR Dost thou call me fool, boy?

FOOL All thy other titles thou hast given away; that thou
wast born with. . . . Prithee, nuncle, keep a schoolmaster
that can teach thy fool to lie: I would fain learn to lie.

LEAR An you lie, sirrah, we'll have you whipped.

This Fool is a recurrent parenthesis, much-beloved of
scholars and dreaded by audiences; he in no way affects
the action, except to impede it, and for a century and a
half the play was performed without him. But he is a
grace-note to Lear, meant in part to accompany him as
a frill of "entertainment"—and doubtless did, when his
pop songs and saws were intelligible to all. He is like no
other person in the play, nearly an abstraction, and with
no life in it except as Lear's shadow he might almost be
the hallucinatory voice of the old man's reason; he will
disappear with it.

Close parenthesis, and enter Goneril with her rebuke
that

> your insolent retinue
> Do hourly carp and quarrel, breaking forth
> In rank and not to be endured riots. Sir,
> I . . . . now grow fearful,
> By what yourself too late have spoke and done,
> That you protect this course and put it on
> By your allowance; which if you should, the fault
> Would not 'scape censure, nor the redresses sleep.

It is not unreasonable, if severe, but it astonishes Lear—
or at least, like an old actor, he plays astonishment for
his followers:

> LEAR   Are you our daughter? . . . .
> Doth any here know me? This is not Lear. . . .
> Who is it that can tell me who I am? . . . .
> Your name, fair gentlewoman?
> GONERIL   This admiration, sir, is much o' the savour
> Of other your new pranks. . . .
> Here do you keep a hundred knights and squires;
> Men so disorder'd, so debosh'd and bold,
> That this our court, infected with their manners,
> Shows . . . . more like a tavern or a brothel
> Than a graced palace. . . . be then desired
> By her that else will take the thing she begs
> A little to disquantity your train. . . .
> To be such men as may besort your age.

Age, yes—"old fools are babes again," she has told us.
This demand is her full move, and it alters Lear as object
remarkably; he is to give up half his hundred, and reacts
as though it were half his testicles.

> LEAR   Darkness and devils!
> Saddle my horses, call my train together.
> Degenerate bastard! I'll not trouble thee:
> Yet have I left a daughter.
> GONERIL   You strike my people, and your disorder'd rabble
> Make servants of their betters. . . .
> LEAR   O Lear, Lear, Lear!
> Beat at this gate, that let thy folly in
> And thy dear judgement out!

And his retaliation is to curse her—in sexual terms, too—
in a rage which has been compared to Yahveh's over his
rebellious children in the wilderness:

Hear, nature, hear. . . .
Suspend thy purpose, if thou didst intend
To make this creature fruitful:
Into her womb convey sterility:
Dry up in her the organs of increase,
And from her derogate body never spring
A babe to honour her! If she must teem,
Create her child of spleen, that it may live
And be a thwart disnatured torment to her.
Let it stamp wrinkles in her brow of youth;
With cadent tears fret channels in her cheeks;
Turn all her mother's pains and benefits
To laughter and contempt; that she may feel
How sharper than a serpent's tooth it is
To have a thankless child!

Lear's view of the matter—"Filial ingratitude!"—is the one taken ever since; we see his play as one of serpent daughters. The evidence thus far has given us only an impossible father, and surely Yahveh's curses are those of a God uncertain of his authority. Lear himself gives us a wider view—

Thou shalt find
That I'll resume the shape which thou dost think
I have cast off for ever—

which is as much that of male competence as of king, and Goneril's counsel to

. . . let his disposition have that scope
That dotage gives it

is a quite appropriate comment on what we have seen; her next move is to dispatch Oswald with a letter of warning to Regan.

To whom Lear now flees, sending Kent ahead with a

letter of his own; his fury is only verbal, like a poet's. It drives him to no counter-move, merely escape to a second apron—"Thou madest thy daughters thy mothers," says the Fool—and whether Lear means the crown when he mutters, "To take't again perforce!" we shall never know, because he never tries. His move is to abandon the battleground. What he does mean is the terrible cry which ends the first act:

> O, let me not be mad, not mad, sweet heaven!
> Keep me in temper: I would not be mad!

So the first chunk of working-out preempts the forestage for Lear's version; the second calls on Edmund for more plot. It picks him up again at Gloucester's castle, with word that Regan and her husband Cornwall are on their way. In this version it is Edmund's move, to "have lands by wit," and Gloucester is its object; now he calls his brother out of hiding—from behind the sofa?—

> O sir, fly this place;
> Intelligence is given where you are hid;
> You have now the good advantage of the night. . . .
> I hear my father coming—

and so pushes him into exile, stabs himself as proof of a struggle, and persuades Gloucester, hurrying in with servants, that Edgar wants him murdered. Active enough, this is hasty machination of no great interest to the playwright, but he is working here in authentic scenes and does not skimp the structure:

> GLOUCESTER   Let him fly far:
>   Not in this land shall he remain uncaught;
>   . . . . and of my land,

> Loyal and natural boy, I'll work the means
> To make thee capable.

Success, the object is altered. But it is only a sop to Edmund's hunger, he will breed further moves, and what this chunk sets up is an unevadable accounting with Edgar. Cornwall, arriving, rewards Edmund by making him his aide. Regan explains the letters have driven them from home; so it is at Gloucester's that the characters from the first chunk too will gather to keep their promises. The two versions have begun at once to interlock, and will soon exchange characters inseparably.

The third chunk is another extended and multiple scene. It opens with a preliminary move by Kent—he is Lear's surrogate—in brawling outside the castle with Oswald for "poisoning" his reception; they are parted by Edmund, and judged by Cornwall:

> CORNWALL　　　　　　　What is his fault?
> KENT　His countenance likes me not.
> CORNWALL　No more perchance does mine. . . .
> KENT　Sir, 'tis my occupation to be plain:
> 　I have seen better faces in my time
> 　Than stands on any shoulder that I see
> 　Before me at this instant.

And Kent as the preliminary move ends up altered, he is locked in the stocks. Regan urges it, a move of hers, and Gloucester's attempt to counter—

> GLOUCESTER　Let me beseech your grace not to do so:
> 　. . . . the king must take it ill,
> 　That he, so slightly valued in his messenger,
> 　Should have him thus restrain'd.
> CORNWALL　　　　　　　　I'll answer that—

is not only a dovetailing of the two stories, moving Gloucester into the fate he and Lear will share; it charges with a new issue the meeting of Lear and Regan, which is the prime promise still overhanging the scene.

Pending which, a parenthesis of twenty-one lines from the other version—numbered as a separate scene by later editors—allows Edgar in flight to tell us

> my face I'll grime with filth,
> Blanket my loins, elf all my hair in knots,
> And with presented nakedness out-face
> The winds and persecutions of the sky,

in order to pass as one of the mad beggars who roam the countryside—because "Edgar I nothing am." True. Until this moment his entire part has totalled nine half-lines; a mere piece set on the board, he is being called to life for the second half, and will hide now from one version in the other.

Lear next arrives, finds Kent in the stocks, learns whose doing it is, is incredulous—

> . . . . down, thou climbing sorrow,
> Thy element's below! Where is this daughter?—

and is refused a meeting. There is a mini-scene between the elders of both versions, with Gloucester as the object—

LEAR Deny to speak with me? They are sick? they are weary?
  They have travell'd all the night? Mere fetches. . . .
  Fetch me a better answer.
GLOUCESTER   My dear lord,
  You know the fiery quality of the duke. . . .
LEAR Fiery? what quality? Why, Gloucester, Gloucester,

I'ld speak with the Duke of Cornwall and his wife.
GLOUCESTER   Well, my good lord, I have inform'd them so.
LEAR   Informed them! Dost thou understand me, man?
GLOUCESTER   Ay, my good lord.
LEAR   The king would speak with Cornwall; the dear father
  Would with his daughter speak, commands her service:
  . . . . bid them come forth and hear me,
  Or at their chamber-door I'll beat the drum
  Till it cry sleep to death—

in which we note Lear is as royal as with Oswald or
Kent; it is only the females who paralyze him, and when
Regan enters he chokes with an old man's tears.

  REGAN   I am glad to see your highness.
  LEAR   . . . . if thou shouldst not be glad,
    I would divorce me from thy mother's tomb,
    Sepulchring an adultress. . . . Beloved Regan,
    Thy sister's naught: O Regan, she hath tied
    Sharp-tooth'd unkindness, like a vulture, here:
    I can scarce speak to thee; thou'lt not believe
    With how deprav'd a quality—O Regan!
  REGAN   I pray you, sir, take patience: I have hope
    You less know how to value her desert
    Than she to scant her duty. . . .
  LEAR   My curses on her!

So Regan tries to reason with him, not impatient until
he kneels before everybody to playact again.

  REGAN   O, sir, you are old;
    Nature in you stands on the very verge
    Of her confine: you should be ruled and led
    By some discretion that discerns your state
    Better than you yourself. Therefore I pray you
    That to our sister you do make return. . . .
  LEAR   Ask her forgiveness?
    Do you but mark how this becomes the house:

101

'Dear daughter, I confess that I am old;
Age is unnecessary: on my knees I beg
That you'll vouchsafe me raiment, bed and food.'
REGAN   Good sir, no more; these are unsightly tricks.

Whereupon Lear rises to such a malevolence that Cornwall too is shocked:

LEAR   All the stored vengeances of heaven fall
On her ingrateful top! Strike her young bones,
You taking airs, with lameness.
CORNWALL   Fie, sir, fie!
LEAR   You nimble lightnings, dart your blinding flames
Into her scornful eyes. Infect her beauty,
You fen-suck'd fogs. . . .
REGAN   O the blest gods! so will you wish on me,
When the rash mood is on.

Indeed. These daughters are short on empathy, but they will not become monsters until the third-act pivot, and then not once in relation to Lear; the evidence is still that of an incontinent old man, and he is demanding

Who stock'd my servant? Regan, I have good hope
Thou didst not know on 't—

when Goneril turns up for the family conclave.

LEAR   Art not ashamed to look upon this beard?
O Regan, will you take her by the hand?

It is Goneril's turn to be astonished; and she again lets fall her unkindest word, too close to home.

GONERIL   Why not by the hand, sir? How have I offended?
All's not offense that indiscretion finds
And dotage terms so.
LEAR   O sides, you are too tough;
Will you yet hold? How came my man i' th' stocks?

CORNWALL   I set him there, sir: but his own disorders
  Deserved much less advancement.
LEAR   You! did you?

There are now three points in play, Goneril, the stocks,
and Lear's waning hope of Regan; she intervenes as
peacemaker, touching again the heart of the matter:

> REGAN   I pray you, father, being weak, seem so.
>   If, till the expiration of your month,
>   You will return and sojourn with my sister,
>   Dismissing half your train, come then to me. . . .
> LEAR   Return to her? . . . .
>   No, rather I abjure all roofs, and choose
>   To wage against the enmity o' the air,
>   To be a comrade with the wolf and owl,—
>   Necessity's sharp pinch! . . .
> GONERIL   At your choice, sir.
> LEAR   I prithee, daughter, do not make me mad. . . .
>   We'll no more meet, no more see one another . . .
>   . . . . I can stay with Regan,
>   I and my hundred knights.

This is his move, which he has ridden all night to make,
and Regan fends it off.

> REGAN   Not altogether so:
>   I look'd not for you yet, nor am provided
>   For your fit welcome. . . . How in one house
>   Should many people under two commands
>   Hold amity? 'Tis hard; almost impossible.

And there ensues the bargaining over the number of his
knights they think tolerable; Regan says twenty-five,
Lear turns back to Goneril whose fifty is "twice her
love," Goneril says her own servants should suffice—
"What need you five and twenty?"—and Regan says,

"What need one?" The move has failed, the object un-altered, and it is Lear who is shattered:

> Oh, reason not the need. . . .
> Allow not nature more than nature needs,
> Man's life's as cheap as beast's. . . .
> You heavens, give me that patience, patience I need!
> You see me here, you gods, a poor old man,
> As full of grief as age; wretched in both:
> . . . . touch me with noble anger,
> And let not women's weapons, water-drops,
> Stain my man's cheeks! No, you unnatural hags,
> I will have such revenges on you both
> That all the world shall—I will do such things—
> What they are, yet I know not; but they shall be
> The terrors of the earth. You think I'll weep;
> No, I'll not weep:
> I have full cause of weeping; but this heart
> Shall break into a hundred thousand flaws,
> Or ere I'll weep. O fool, I shall go mad!

It has begun to storm, and he runs out into it.

It is the last choice he makes in the play. Hidden in such convoluted scenework and the bold colors of the role, the moves Lear makes in the working-out add up to two—he flees from one daughter, flees from the other—and are childishly simple; now he will only suffer. But we are barely out of the second act. Who is capable of extending the play?

Now we can see why the double plot; the need is dis-cernible by hindsight in each exposition itself. Lear in the first scene has created a set of antagonists, good daughter, loyal servitor, bad daughters, and the next moves must be theirs; his are for the moment exhausted. But there has arisen a problem with their moves. Cordelia is married and off to France, out of the play; Kent can return in disguise to serve Lear, but cannot undo his folly; and Regan and Goneril, already possessed of his kingdom, have no further object other than to ward off the old porcupine. And our eye is on him, one against many—the master promise, implied, is Lear's redress of his general injustice. But the barrier to it is his paranoid vision of them all, "the infirmity of his age," and here we are beyond the reach of human will. It is a barrier which events, not Lear, must break down; he can only suffer the events. In this version, then, the principle is passive.

It is in the other exposition that Edmund—"All with me's meet that I can fashion"—has initiated another master promise, not implied, and the barrier is only "a credulous father, and a brother noble"; no problem with the moves here, they are solely Edmund's and far from exhausted. In this version, then, the principle is active.

The mirroring of the two versions is deceptive. Overtly duplicates, Lear's version has a formidable barrier in him and no effective move, Gloucester's a formidable move in Edmund and no effective barrier; in their dynamics, the stories *are* opposites. And neither by itself would suffice. The playwright is now interfitting these two imperfect half-plays into a whole, building on a common theme; it is an immense canon. Who is capable of extending the play?—only Edmund, and his version will keep the movement active around Lear passive, while time and events undo the barrier of his insanity. This much of the mirroring is the playwright's solution structurally; by the third-act pivot we shall see what he does with it thematically.

The third of course is the unforgettable act, scenes
and characters leapfrogging till the two versions are in-
extricable. It opens with Kent in the storm on the heath,
searching for the King and doing state business too; he
has news—here is a story-point—that "a power from
France" has landed, and dispatches word to Cordelia at
its head. It is perhaps the archetypal nature of the action
that keeps us from noting we now face a civil war because Goneril has objected to too many house-guests.
The storm itself is archetypal—Kent tells us

> since I was man,
> Such sheets of fire, such bursts of horrid thunder,
> Such groans of roaring wind and rain, I never
> Remember to have heard—

and so is the histrionic figure of Lear in dialogue with it,
screaming words at the tortured edge of language:

LEAR Blow, winds, and crack your cheeks! rage! blow!
  You cataracts and hurricanoes, spout
  Till you have drench'd our steeples, drown'd the cocks!
  You sulphurous and thought-executing fires,
  Vaunt-couriers to oak-cleaving thunderbolts,
  Singe my white head! And thou, all-shaking thunder,
  Strike flat the thick rotundity o' the world!
  Crack nature's moulds, all germens spill at once
  That make ingrateful man!
FOOL O nuncle. . . . in and ask thy daughters' blessing:
  here's a night pities neither wise man nor fool.
LEAR Rumble thy bellyful! Spit, fire! spout, rain!
  . . . . Let the great gods,
  That keep this dreadful pother o'er our heads,
  Find out their enemies now. Tremble, thou wretch,
  That hast within thee undivulged crimes. . . .

Kent leads them to a nearby hovel; and on the brink of lunacy Lear—have the gods heard?—for the first time feels for someone other than himself:

> My wits begin to turn.
> Come on, my boy: how dost, my boy? art cold? . . . .
> Poor fool and knave, I have one part in my heart
> That's sorry yet for thee.

Back to Edmund, who in a scene with his father learns he also has news of Cordelia's invasion.

GLOUCESTER . . . . 'tis dangerous to be spoken; I have locked the letter in my closet: these injuries the king now bears will be revenged home. . . .

This old man's move is to look for the other old man and "relieve him, if I die for it," which he will; and it puts into Edmund's hand the move that propels the play to its third-act pivot, he will inform on Gloucester

> and of that letter too:
> This seems a fair deserving, and must draw me
> That which my father loses; no less than all:
> The younger rises when the old doth fall.

Young and old, it is a fact of life, grimmer than ingratitude.

Back to Lear in the storm outside the hovel, where he lingers to

> pray, and then I'll sleep.
> Poor naked wretches, wheresoe'er you are,
> That bide the pelting of this pitiless storm,
> How shall your houseless heads and unfed sides,
> Your loop'd and window'd raggedness, defend you

> From seasons such as these? Oh, I have ta'en
> Too little care of this!

This storm, without, within, is the tutor Regan said he needed—

> to wilful men
> The injuries that they themselves procure
> Must be their schoolmasters—

and he is learning fast, peeling off royal ego, but with a cracking mind; we are watching it go, scene by scene. Thus, when Edgar as a demented beggar comes out of the hovel, jabbering and naked:

LEAR   What, have his daughters brought him to this pass?
   Couldst thou save nothing? Didst thou give them all?
FOOL   Nay, he reserved a blanket, else we had been all shamed. . . .
LEAR   Thou wert better in thy grave than to answer with thy uncovered body this extremity of the skies. Is man no more than this? . . . . Ha! here's three on 's are sophisticated. Thou art the thing itself: unaccommodated man is no more but such a poor, bare, forked animal as thou art. Off, off, you lendings! come, unbutton here.

In now comes Gloucester on his move, a "walking fire" with his torch in the storm; he recognizes neither Kent nor Edgar in disguise.

GLOUCESTER   . . . . I ventured to come seek you out
   And bring you where both fire and food is ready.
LEAR   First let me talk with this philosopher.
   What is the cause of thunder? . . . .
KENT   His wits begin to unsettle.
GLOUCESTER   Canst thou blame him?
   His daughters seek his death . . .

It is a startling charge. There is not an iota of evidence to support it; we have combed the play for their behavior to Lear up to this point, and seen it loveless but no worse. And the incredible fact is that after the second act this pair of patricides between them devote exactly one line to their father—they are too busy wrestling over Edmund, who will be the death of them. No; Gloucester, having crossed the boundary, is confusing which version he is in—

> I am almost mad myself: I had a son,
> Now outlaw'd from my blood; he sought my life,
> But lately, very late: I loved him, friend,
> No father his son dearer: true to tell thee,
> The grief hath crazed my wits—

and has misled us all into taking his crazed view as the playwright's.

Back to Edmund, who in the interval has lost no time in making sure the "old doth fall"—

CORNWALL   I will have my revenge ere I depart his house.

EDMUND   How, my lord, I may be censured, that nature thus gives way to loyalty, something fears me to think of.

CORNWALL   I now perceive, it was not altogether your brother's evil disposition made him seek his death. . . .

EDMUND   How malicious is my fortune, that I must repent to be just! This is the letter he spoke of, which approves him an intelligent party to the advantages of France. . . .

CORNWALL   True or false, it hath made thee earl of Gloucester. Seek out where thy father is, that he may be ready for our apprehension.

The act is turning toward Gloucester now. It gives us one glimpse more of Lear, quite daft, hallucinating a trial in Gloucester's farmhouse—

LEAR   Arraign her first; 'tis Goneril. I here take my oath before this honourable assembly, she kicked the poor king her father.

FOOL   Come hither, mistress. Is your name Goneril?

LEAR   She cannot deny it.

FOOL   Cry you mercy, I took you for a joint-stool—

before the other old worthy hurries him out again toward Dover; then it reverts to inside the castle, where Gloucester himself is the quarry. And suddenly both daughters are harpies:

CORNWALL   . . . the army of France is landed. Seek out the traitor Gloucester.

REGAN   Hang him instantly.

GONERIL   Pluck out his eyes.

This being "not fit for your beholding," Edmund must escort Goneril on the road home; so is born their romance. Gloucester is now brought in.

CORNWALL   Bind fast his corky arms.

GLOUCESTER   What mean your graces? Good my friends, consider
   You are my guests. . . .

CORNWALL   Bind him, I say.

REGAN   Hard, hard. . . .

CORNWALL   Come sir, what letters had you late from France?

REGAN   Be simple-answer'd, for we know the truth.

CORNWALL   And what confederacy have you with the traitors
   Late footed in the kingdom?

REGAN   To whose hands have you sent the lunatic king? . . . .

GLOUCESTER   To Dover.

There is the one line about their father; the issue is no longer filial, it is one of life-and-death in the teeth of a foreign invasion, a new game and deadlier stakes. And Gloucester's conjecture, self-referential again, is as wild as Lear's curse:

GLOUCESTER   Because I would not see thy cruel nails
    Pluck out his poor old eyes, nor thy fierce sister
    In his anointed flesh stick boarish fangs. . . .
CORNWALL   See 't shalt thou never. Fellows, hold the chair.
    Upon these eyes of thine I'll set my foot.
GLOUCESTER   He that will think to live till he be old,
    Give me some help! O cruel! O you gods!
REGAN   One side will mock another; the other too.

Here a servant—one who hopes to "be old" too—rebels, draws on Cornwall, wounds him, and is killed by Regan; Cornwall then gouges out Gloucester's other eye.

CORNWALL   Out, vile jelly!
    Where is thy luster now?
GLOUCESTER   All dark and comfortless. . . .
REGAN   Go thrust him out at gates, and let him smell
    His way to Dover.

So the third-act pivot, and it is a nightmare. It has made the two stories one by splitting the characters of each version into successes and failures, and brought the successes together in the castle, and spilled the failures out into the most apocalyptic storm in literature; and in each version it has singled out the old dignitary and wrecked him. The one in mind, the other in body. It has pulled Lear down from his imperious authority into the fumblings of a senile psychotic, and thrown Gloucester out after him to grope his way with bleeding sockets in the storm; they will next meet as madman and attempted suicide.

   If we read the third-act pivot as expressive of theme,

what is the double image here crying out?—old age, loss of powers, impotence, death-in-life, the wreckage of mind and body in time; and the playwright tells the same story twice to make, not a special, but a universal case. Thus too the sexual undercurrent—Lear recoils from "the sulphurous pit" below the female girdle, and Edmund as the active principle in youth will conquer both daughters of the passive in age. This is not a play about the fifth commandment, it is after something immutable, and the ingratitude of children is only tributary to it.

15. *Aside*

Our subject grows more and more complex; what began as a simple examination of craft—how does our greatest playwright lay out his material?—is leading us into a multitudinous tangle of questions about art and its creation. I did say the distinction fails when craft becomes form, it then is inseparable from art. And willy-nilly we have long since crossed the line; we are in the thick of character emerging from scenework, and of language, mood, tempo emerging from character, and of meaning emerging from all in the third-act pivot. The wealth of these plays is infinite, and we must circumscribe our subject somewhere.

Let us here touch on a world we shall not really enter, the nature of character and its relation to that structure of contradictions we call a play.

For Iago the barrier is outward, external to him—the enigma here is his psychic unity. To the question, Why is he so empty of conflict about his evil? we can answer only that it is the given of the play, a postulate of undivided will. Not so with Othello, he is divided inwardly and fatally between his needs to love and to destroy, and there is where the tragedy lies; struggle between a character wholly good and one wholly evil is for children. With Othello we are back to the interesting turn we observed in Angelo, where a struggle between two wills becomes an inner struggle in one, and we shall look into Othello's later.

It is a dimension lacking in Richard III, he is like Iago with no Othello, and the play is the shallower for it. But what is it in Shylock that fascinates us?—not his vengefulness for his ducats, if that were all of him he would be only a "humor," like many characters of Shakespeare's lesser contemporaries now extinct as matchsticks; it is both that *and* his proud "sufferance, the badge of all our tribe" which constitutes his humanity; the inner contradiction makes him live. What is it in Macbeth?—the struggle with his own dread over his "fated" murders. Why is the surrogate sleepwalking of his Lady so unforgettable?—

GENTLEWOMAN   It is an accustomed action with her, to seem thus washing of her hands: I have known her to continue in this a quarter of an hour.

LADY MACBETH   Yet here's a spot.

DOCTOR   Hark! she speaks. . . .

LADY MACBETH   Out, damned spot! out, I say! One: two: why, then, 'tis time to do 't. Hell is murky. Fie, my lord, fie! a soldier, and afeard? . . . . Yet who would have thought the old man to have had so much blood in him?

DOCTOR   Do you mark that?

LADY MACBETH   . . . . What, will these hands ne'er be clean? No more o' that, my lord, no more o' that: you mar all with this starting.

GENTLEWOMAN   . . . . Heaven knows what she has known.

114

LADY MACBETH   Here's the smell of the blood still: all the
perfumes of Arabia will not sweeten this little hand. Oh,
oh, oh!

DOCTOR   What a sigh is there! The heart is sorely charged.

GENTLEWOMAN   I would not have such a heart in my bosom
for the dignity of the whole body. . . .

LADY MACBETH   Wash your hands; put on your nightgown;
look not so pale: I'll tell you yet again, Banquo's buried;
he cannot come out on 's grave.

DOCTOR   Even so?

LADY MACBETH   To bed, to bed; there's knocking at the
gate: come, come, come, come, give me your hand: what's
done cannot be undone: to bed, to bed, to bed—

because it is compounded of the same inner war between
daring and guilt; half her words are her husband's, the
conflict between them is now in her.

Here is a scenelet from the second act of *Antony and
Cleopatra*, which delivers a mere story-point, word of
Antony's marriage. See how it becomes a drama of character in which, in the space of five minutes, this irides-
cent queen is at first playful—

> I will betray
> Tawny-finn'd fishes; my bended hook shall pierce
> Their slimy jaws, and as I draw them up,
> I'll think them every one an Antony,
> And say, 'Ah, ha! you're caught'—

then bawdy as a man—

> O, from Italy!
> Ram thou thy fruitful tidings in mine ears,
> That long time have been barren.
> MESSENGER   Madam, madam—

then fearful as a bird—

    CLEOPATRA   Antonius dead! If thou say so, villain,
    Thou kill'st thy mistress—

then sensual as a harlot—

                  but well and free,
     If thou so yield him, there is gold, and here
     My bluest veins to kiss—

and vain—

                  a hand that kings
    Have lipp'd, and trembled kissing.
    MESSENGER   First, madam, he is well.
    CLEOPATRA   Why, there's more gold.
    But, sirrah, mark, we use
    To say the dead are well—

and cruel—

                  bring it to that,
    The gold I give thee will I melt and pour
    Down thy ill-uttering throat—

and shrewd—

    MESSENGER   Good madam, hear me.
    CLEOPATRA   Well, go to, I will;
    But there's no goodness in thy face. . . .
    MESSENGER   Will 't please you hear me?—

and wilful—

    CLEOPATRA   I have a mind to strike thee ere thou speak'st:
    Yet, if thou say Antony lives, is well,
    Or friends with Caesar, or not captive to him—

and prodigal—

        I'll set thee in a shower of gold, and hail
        Rich pearls upon thee.
    MESSENGER   Madam, he's well—

and serene—

CLEOPATRA   Well said.
MESSENGER   And friends with Caesar.
CLEOPATRA   Thou'rt an honest man.
MESSENGER   Caesar and he are greater friends than ever.
CLEOPATRA   Make thee a fortune from me.
MESSENGER   But yet, madam—

and apprehensive—

    CLEOPATRA   I do not like 'But yet,' it does allay
    The good precedence—

and self-controlled—

                    Prithee, friend,
Pour out the pack of matter to mine ear,
The good and bad together: he's friends with Caesar,
In state of health, thou say'st, and thou say'st, free.
MESSENGER   Free, madam; no; I made no such report:
He's bound unto Octavia.
CLEOPATRA   For what good turn?
MESSENGER   For the best turn i' the bed.
CLEOPATRA   I am pale, Charmian.

—what an extraordinary remark!—

    MESSENGER   Madam, he's married to Octavia—

and raging—

CLEOPATRA   The most infectious pestilence upon thee!
                        Strikes him down
MESSENGER   Good madam, patience.
CLEOPATRA   What say you? Hence,
                        Strikes him again
Horrible villain! or I'll spurn thine eyes
Like balls before me; I'll unhair thy head!
                Hales him up and down

Thou shalt be whipp'd with wire, and stew'd in brine,
Smarting in lingering pickle.
MESSENGER   Gracious madam,
I that do bring the news made not the match—

and pleading—

CLEOPATRA   Say 'tis not so, a province I will give thee
And make thy fortunes proud. . . .
MESSENGER   He's married, madam—

and murderous—

CLEOPATRA   Rogue! thou hast lived too long.

Draws a knife

MESSENGER   Nay, then I'll run. . . .

Exit

CHARMIAN   Good madam, keep yourself within yourself:
The man is innocent—

and olympian—

CLEOPATRA   Some innocents 'scape not the thunderbolt—

and reasonable—

Call the slave again:
Though I am mad, I will not bite him: call.
CHARMIAN   He is afeard to come.
CLEOPATRA   I will not hurt him—

and self-condemning—

These hands do lack nobility, that they strike
A meaner than myself; since I myself
Have given myself the cause—

and calm—

Come hither, sir.
Though it be honest, it is never good

118

  To bring bad news. . . .

MESSENGER   I have done my duty.

CLEOPATRA   Is he married?

  I cannot hate thee worser than I do

  If thou again say 'Yes.'

MESSENGER   He's married, madam—

and furious—

CLEOPATRA   The gods confound thee! dost thou hold there
  still?

MESSENGER   Should I lie, madam?

CLEOPATRA   O! I would thou didst.

  . . . . Go, get thee hence:

  Hadst thou Narcissus in thy face, to me

  Thou wouldst appear most ugly—

and stunned—

                 He is married?

MESSENGER   I crave your highness' pardon.

CLEOPATRA   He is married?

MESSENGER   Take no offence that I would not offend you:

  To punish me for what you make me do

  Seems much unequal: he's married to Octavia—

and waspish—

  CLEOPATRA   Get thee hence:

  The merchandise which thou hast brought from Rome

  Are all too dear for me: lie they upon thy hand

  And be undone by 'em—

and frail—

               Lead me from hence;

               I faint—

and very feminine—

> bid him
> Report the feature of Octavia, her years,
> Her inclination; let him not leave out
> The colour of her hair: bring me word quickly—

and torn—

> Let him for ever go; let him not—Charmian,
> Though he be painted one way like a Gorgon,
> The other way's a Mars—

and pathetic—

> Bring me word how tall she is—

and proud—

> Pity me, Charmian,
> But do not speak to me. Lead me to my chamber.

How this creature on a page *breathes*!—and all this dazzle of contradictory colors takes place within a greater contradiction, that of an imperious queen made helpless by love; her thrashing between these two incompatibles creates the scene.

> I myself
> Have given myself the cause,

which is the inner contradiction that makes every character live. But then each is a drama in himself, of moves toward objects through barriers, all internal; the opposites of the soul are the antagonists, and this conflict like others makes itself visible only in action. The move is again the microstructure, of character too.

That said, we are ready to return to Hamlet.

16. *The Inner Contradiction*

We left him at the first-act curtain in a dismay—
"The time is out of joint"—that twists his thoughts inward, "O cursed spite, that ever I was born," and outward, "to set it right." For Hamlet the barrier is always
twofold, it first divides him and the King, and then
halves of himself; and it is partly for this reason "the"
play of the modern world.

Its enigmas are many. The attracting and keeping
apart of each of its pairs of opposites, the outer and the
inner, makes for a fourfold complexity in the intervening matter; easily felt, this is difficult enough to unravel
on the wing. But this complexity is itself confused by a
text whose trustworthiness, in consecutivity of scenes, is
suspect—of that, more later. Meanwhile, the working-out
in its next two acts invites our eyes to follow it move by
move; it is itself fascinating, and separating the double
braid of its barrier may help elucidate some of the
enigmas.

The constellation of the three principal characters
forms what we have called the basic triangle of the play;
from Hamlet's corner, one line leads to the King, the

other to his mother. Unlike a triangle, the two lines intertwine in counterpoint, but each consists of a working-out which may be viewed separately.

First, the line from Hamlet to the King.

The barrier between them is a reciprocal uncertainty; Hamlet is not sure what the King has done, and the King is not sure what Hamlet knows. Nor are we. Our only informant is the ghost, and although at first flush Hamlet says

> Touching this vision here,
> It is an honest ghost, that let me tell you,

he is of another mind the next time we see him:

> The spirit that I have seen
> May be the devil; and the devil hath power
> To assume a pleasing shape; yea, and perhaps. . . .
> Abuses me to damn me. I'll have grounds
> More relative than this.

Or, corroboration. So the barrier, *his* uncertainty, is what draws the master move and object closer—his intermediate object now is to know "the conscience of the King." But even this object is out of reach, until he finds the means.

The ghost's tale however has shaken him; and if true, knowing it sets him up as the next target. How to stand "out of the shot and danger"? In the original tale, the character feigns a drooling kind of idiocy, like David's with the king of Gath, to seem harmless; and this is what Hamlet, creating one of the enigmas, at first promises:

HORATIO   Propose the oath, my lord.
HAMLET   Never to speak of this that you have seen. . . .
    How strange or odd soe'er I bear myself,

As I perchance hereafter shall think meet
To put an antic disposition on—

but his "wild and whirling words" before this were un-premeditated. Hearsay is what we have next, Ophelia's report—

> his doublet all unbrac'd,
> No hat upon his head, his stockings foul'd. . . .
> Pale as his shirt, his knees knocking each other,
> And with a look so piteous in purport
> As if he had been loosed out of hell
> To speak of horrors, he comes before me—

which her father takes as the "very ecstasy of love"; we may take it as either genuine or the antic disposition, put on to be reported back. Why?—in the original, "wallow-ing and lying in the durt . . . he seemed fitte for noth-ing but to make sport to the pages," and so stayed alive; but if this is our Hamlet's motive not a word corrobo-rates it. We are never told why he thinks it "meet." If his intent is to seem harmless, his antics—shouting insults at all the court, putting on tactless plays, stabbing through curtains at old folks—are so obstreperous that even an innocent king would get rid of him.

Others now speak of his "transformation," "lunacy," "distemper," but what do we ourselves see onstage?—only his savage bantering with Polonius, who himself finds "method in 't," and his sudden savagery with Ophelia, who judges

> a noble mind is here o'erthrown! . . . .
> Like sweet bells jangled out of tune

because it tongue-lashes her, with utmost relevance, for serving as her father's bait. We have seen with Lear how misleading the testimony of other characters can be; Hamlet's own is—

HAMLET My uncle-father and my aunt-mother are deceived.
GUILDENSTERN In what, my dear lord?
HAMLET I am but mad north-north-west; when the wind is southerly I know a hawk from a handsaw—

and later—

HAMLET Sir, I cannot.
GUILDENSTERN What, my lord?
HAMLET Make you a wholesome answer; my wit's diseased.

Which is hardly persuasive. To his mother he says—

> Ecstasy!
> My pulse, as yours, doth temperately keep time,
> And makes as healthful music: it is not madness
> That I have utter'd: bring me to the test,
> And I the matter will re-word, which madness
> Would gambol from,

and proves it by the sanity of

> Mother, for love of grace,
> Lay not that flattering unction to your soul,
> That not your trespass but my madness speaks:
> It will but skin and film the ulcerous place,
> Whilst rank corruption, mining all within,
> Infects unseen.

All the more confusing is his fifth-act apology to Laertes—

> you must needs have heard, how I am punish'd
> With sore distraction. What I have done
> . . . . I here proclaim was madness—

124

a speech thrown out of the play by one editor who could not stomach such a falsehood as genuine Bard. Can Hamlet, the very hound of truth, mean it? His thinking is never impaired; the passion behind it is wild, at times hysterical. On the other hand, why not?—his plight is not average, he lives at the breaking-point. On the third hand, playacting is not so separable from psychosis, as psychiatrists know; we have noted it in Lear also.

Is Hamlet mad or feigning?—neither view can be maintained without excluding contrary evidence in the play. The question itself is irrational, it confounds an artwork and life; all we can ask into is the playwright's intention. "Frantic mad with evermore unrest" is how he sonnetized of his own state, in love; it would serve Hamlet, in worse straits. The question would not arise except for Hamlet's promising the device of the original tale, and the playwright has aborted its use.

In any case, he is certainly upset, and the King sees it. Solicitous or fearful?—either way it is again the barrier, *his* uncertainty, which draws the master object and move closer. The King makes the next two moves, which are in intent identical. The first is a "hasty sending" for Rosencrantz and Guildenstern to spy on their friend, and report whether anything "to us unknown afflicts him thus"; the second is to let Polonius "loose" his daughter on her royal beau, while her father and the King eavesdrop.

The first move, Hamlet sees through almost at once— "I know the good king and queen have sent for you"— and his friends learn nothing from him except that "man delights not me"; but from them he learns of the players, en route to the castle, and he finds his means. It is his own second move, to have them play "something like the murder of my father" with lines which he will add to "catch the conscience of the king." When Rosencrantz and Guildenstern report back his "kind of joy" in the coming play, the King approves of "these delights."

The eavesdropping, Hamlet sees through midway in a conversation which begins

> Nymph, in thy orisons
> Be all my sins remember'd,

and continues gentle until

HAMLET   Where's your father?
OPHELIA   At home, my lord.
HAMLET   Let the doors be shut upon him, that he may play the fool no where but in 's own house—

and, betrayed now by his love, turns his berating of her into a loud threat intelligible only to the King himself:

I say, we will have no more marriages: those that are married already, all but one, shall live.

The King thinks him not at all harmless—"he shall with speed to England."

The King's two traps have been sprung, and caught only this shadow; Hamlet's now takes over. The play is given before the assembled court. Hamlet "rivets" his eyes on the King; he has earlier said that if his uncle's

> guilt
> Do not unkennel itself in one speech,
> It is a damned ghost that we have seen,
> And my imaginations are as foul
> As Vulcan's stithy.

But they are not: the moment "one Lucianus" pours poison into the Player King's ear, all is consternation.

> OPHELIA   The king rises.
> HAMLET   What, frighted with false fire!
> QUEEN   How fares my lord?
> POLONIUS   Give o'er the play.
> KING   Give me some light. Away!
> ALL   Lights, lights, lights!

And in the scene immediately following the King, alone at prayer, confesses:

> O, my offence is rank, it smells to heaven;
> It hath the primal eldest curse upon 't,
> A brother's murder.

The uncertainty is ended—we know now, Hamlet knows, and the King knows Hamlet knows—so when Hamlet coming upon him draws his sword, there is no barrier between them. Outwardly. The moment has come for the sword to join the master move and object, ending the play. But Hamlet puts it up, unused. Ostensibly, because to kill the King at prayer will "this same villain send to heaven"; better to wait till he is "in the incestuous pleasure of his bed." Actually, because Hamlet has a more urgent topic to take up with his mother, and it is precisely that "incestuous" pleasure:

> My mother stays:
> This physic but prolongs thy sickly days.

What keeps the master move and object apart now is a dividedness in Hamlet himself; the true barrier is inward.

So, the line from Hamlet to his mother.

It begins with his first words in the play—"A little

more than kin"—in repudiation of her new mate; a moment later he is hinting at the hypocrisy of her mourning—

> Seems, madam! nay, it is; I know not "seems."
> 'Tis not alone my inky cloak, good mother,
> Nor customary suits of solemn black—

and nine words later it is all tumbling out, in the first soliloquy. This opening manifesto equates his nausea for the world,

> an unweeded garden,
> That grows to seed; things rank and gross in nature
> Possess it merely,

with his nausea for his mother's

> most wicked speed, to post
> With such dexterity to incestuous sheets!—

to sound the ground-bass of his thought, incest. The word will stick to him like a loathsome burr. Main melody—the pursuit of ghost and King: Horatio is in at once—will drown it out; this is, after all, a tragedy of revenge.

HORATIO   I came to see your father's funeral.
HAMLET   . . . . I think it was to see my mother's wedding.
HORATIO   Indeed, my lord, it follow'd hard upon.
HAMLET   . . . . Would I had met my dearest foe in heaven
   Or ever I had seen that day!

Or is it?

From the ghost he learns of two offences; first,

> that adulterate beast
> . . . . won to his shameful lust
> The will of my most seeming-virtuous queen,

and second,

> stole,
> With juice of cursed hebenon in a vial,
> And in the porches of my ears did pour
> The leperous distilment.

It is only the murder Hamlet is to avenge; on the adultery the ghost is explicit—

> nor let thy soul contrive
> Against thy mother aught: leave her to heaven—

and Hamlet swears

> thy commandment all alone shall live
> Within the book and volume of my brain,
> Unmix'd with baser matter.

What baser matter?—he ranks the offenders thus,

> O most pernicious woman!
> O villain, villain, smiling, damned villain!—

and not once in this play will he think of the murder unmix'd with the adultery, the King is always "bloody, bawdy" and "treacherous, lecherous"; they are equal crimes.

Obedient to the ghost, he has no overt move now against his mother; but his preoccupation surfaces in idle conversation—

GUILDENSTERN   On Fortune's cap we are not the very button.
HAMLET   Nor the soles of her shoe?
ROSENCRANTZ   Neither, my lord.
HAMLET   Then you live about her waist, or in the middle of her favours?
GUILDENSTERN   Faith, her privates we.

HAMLET   In the secret parts of Fortune? O, most true; she
  is a strumpet—

and when later in the scene he asks a speech of the strolling players his choice is not random, albeit a bit spinachy in style:

HAMLET   . . . . say on: come to Hecuba.
PLAYER   'But who, O, who had seen the mobled queen. . . .
  Run barefoot up and down, threatening the flames
  With bisson rheum; a clout upon that head
  Where late the diadem stood; and for a robe,
  About her lank and all o'er-teemed loins,
  A blanket, in the alarm of fear caught up. . . .
  When she saw Pyrrhus make malicious sport
  In mincing with his sword her husband's limbs,
  The instant burst of clamour that she made. . . .'

It is a tribute—"one speech in it I chiefly loved"—to a loyal and grief-stricken wife. The Queen is his covert theme in the whole scene with Ophelia, both its quiet half—

. . . the power of beauty will sooner transform honesty from what it is to a bawd than the force of honesty can translate beauty into his likeness: this was sometime a paradox, but now the time gives it proof—

and its noisy—

Get thee to a nunnery, go. . . . Or, if thou wilt needs marry, marry a fool; for wise men know well enough what monsters you make of them. . . .

—that is, horned, like his father—

God has given you one face, and you make yourselves another: you jig, you amble, and you lisp. . . . and make your wantonness your ignorance. . . . it hath made me mad,

and he threatens the royal pair—is it only the King?—with death.

Now he is ready with his play to trap him; the third act is building inexorably to the enormous question, Is the King guilty? and Hamlet is on tenterhooks for the answer; what is his conversation?

HAMLET   Do you think I meant country matters?
OPHELIA   I think nothing, my lord.
HAMLET   That's a fair thought to lie between maids' legs.
OPHELIA   What is, my lord?
HAMLET   Nothing.
OPHELIA   You are merry, my lord. . . .
HAMLET   O God, your only jig-maker. What should a man do but be merry? for, look you, how cheerfully my mother looks, and my father died within 's two hours.
OPHELIA   Nay, 'tis twice two months.

Immediately after:

HAMLET   Is this a prologue? . . . .
OPHELIA   'Tis brief, my lord.
HAMLET   As woman's love.

Thirty lines into the performance:

PLAYER QUEEN   'In second husband let me be accurst!
None wed the second but who kill'd the first.'
HAMLET (*aside*)   Wormwood, wormwood,

—the first intimation that his mother may be party to his father's murder—

PLAYER QUEEN   'Both here and hence pursue me lasting strife,

If, once a widow, ever I be wife!'
HAMLET   If she should break it now! . . . . Madam, how
like you this play?
QUEEN   The lady protests too much, methinks.
HAMLET   O, but she'll keep her word.

But surely this play is aimed rather at the King?—yes,
and now occur two unnecessary and remarkable touches.
We have been led first into a parallel between the Player
King and Hamlet's father; enter the poisoner. Of course
it is his uncle the King?—no, Hamlet himself identifies
him as

This is one Lucianus, nephew to the king.

Nephew!—the whole parallel is altered; now the Player
King is the uncle, the poisoner is Hamlet, and the play
is not re-enactment but threat. And what he offers next
is more startling:

. . . you shall see anon how the murderer gets the love of
Gonzago's wife.

In the first parallel, fact, his uncle gets the love of his
father's wife; in the second, wish, the nephew gets the
love of his uncle's wife; the two parallels have blurred
in one contamination, and the only character identical
in both is Hamlet's mother.

Meanwhile the "play" proceeds, the king is hit and
flees:

HAMLET   O good Horatio, I'll take the ghost's word for a
thousand pounds. Didst perceive?
HORATIO   Very well, my lord.
HAMLET   Upon the talk of the poisoning?
HORATIO   I did very well note him.
HAMLET   Ah, ha! Come, some music!

And that is all. Alone with his brooding, Hamlet opens himself to us:

> 'Tis now the very witching time of night,
> When churchyards yawn, and hell itself breathes out
> Contagion to this world: now could I drink hot blood,
> And do such bitter business as the day
> Would quake to look on. Soft! now to my mother.

To his *mother*?

> O heart, lose not thy nature; let not ever
> The soul of Nero enter this firm bosom:
> Let me be cruel, not unnatural:
> I will speak daggers to her, but use none—

A bizarre imbalance is taking place, as we near the third-act pivot; the ground-bass is rising to drown out the melody.

With the next scene Hamlet's move to kill the King comes, and he walks past it; this is not the pivot. Instead his move is into the Queen's bedchamber, where Polonius is hidden to eavesdrop—

HAMLET Now, mother, what's the matter?
QUEEN Hamlet, thou hast thy father much offended.
HAMLET Mother, you have my father much offended.
QUEEN Come, come, you answer with an idle tongue.
HAMLET Go, go, you question with a wicked tongue. . . .
QUEEN Have you forgot me?
HAMLET   No, by the rood, not so:
  You are the queen, your husband's brother's wife;
  And—would it were not so!—you are my mother.
QUEEN Nay, then, I'll set those to you that can speak.
HAMLET Come, come, and sit you down; you shall not budge;
  You go not till I set you up a glass

Where you may see the inmost part of you.
QUEEN   What will thou do? thou wilt not murder me?
Help, help, ho!—

and Polonius joins in her cry; Hamlet stabs him through
the curtain, but this is not the pivot.

QUEEN   O me, what hast thou done?
HAMLET   Nay, I know not: is it the king?
QUEEN   O, what a rash and bloody deed is this!
HAMLET   A bloody deed! almost as bad, good mother,
   As kill a king, and marry with his brother.
QUEEN   As kill a king!
HAMLET   Ay, lady, 'twas my word.

There is one tacit pronoun common to "kill" and
"marry." Now we are at the very center of the web we
have watched Hamlet spin for three acts; the King's
guilt is known, and the only question in the world for
Hamlet is, Were you his accomplice in my father's
murder?

He forgets to ask it. He forgets in fact that the murder has happened; he sits her down and charges her with

                    Such an act
   That blurs the grace and blush of modesty,
   Calls virtue hypocrite, takes off the rose
   From the fair forehead of an innocent love,
   And sets a blister there; makes marriage vows
   As false as dicers' oaths: O, such a deed
   As from the body of contraction plucks
   The very soul, and sweet religion makes
   A rhapsody of words: heaven's face doth glow;
   Yea, this solidity and compound mass,
   With tristful visage, as against the doom,
   Is thought-sick at the act—

134

by which he means the earth itself—and she is amazed; his charge is not murder, but lust. It is by now the worse crime, and he denounces her for it as he has ached to do since his first scene, working a spiritual rape until she cries for mercy:

> These words like daggers enter in mine ears;
> No more, sweet Hamlet!

Enter the ghost, to remind Hamlet of his non-existence, and to make peace between his Queen and son. Hamlet is calmed—

> QUEEN O Hamlet, thou hast cleft my heart in twain.
> HAMLET   O, throw away the worser part of it,
>   And live the purer with the other half.
>   Good night; but go not to mine uncle's bed—

and after more picturing of the lustful delights she is to forgo, he drags Polonius out; not another word of murder or revenge, he will obey the King, who is packing him off to England.

This is the third-act pivot; what does it tell us?

Hamlet is often explained—another enigma—as too intellectual to "act"; it is his own comment in soliloquy:

> Thus conscience does make cowards of us all,
> And thus the native hue of resolution
> Is sicklied o'er with the pale cast of thought,
> And enterprises of great pitch and moment
> With this regard their currents turn awry
> And lose the name of action.

This word "coward" is in three of the five major soliloquies, and implied in all—

>   Am I a coward?
> Who calls me villain? . . .

'Swounds, I should take it: for it cannot be
But I am pigeon-liver'd—

             Now, whether it be
Bestial oblivion, or some craven scruple
Of thinking too precisely on the event,—
A thought which, quarter'd, hath but one part wisdom
And ever three parts coward,—

and we have taken him at his word. But "to act"?—this
is a young man who challenges ghosts his soldiers fear,
taunts all his betters, stages plays in full court to expose
its king, kills instantly, boards pirate ships in combat,
sends schoolmates to their deaths without a scruple, leaps
into graves to grapple with homicidal brothers—he is the
least inhibited hero in drama, and only the brilliant play
of his intelligence obscures that datum. Why does he
hesitate at the King?

Practically?—to keep the play alive, of course, it has
two acts to go; we sometimes forget that his author is
writing to make a living. Psychologically?—because, as
the third-act pivot tells us, he is not after the King; he is
after his mother. The King is antagonist only on his own
level; on Hamlet's, he is a surrogate.

It is an extraordinary moment. A protagonist, making
his move through a deadly barrier to his object, finds the
encounter is empty; only then, he turns in an unplanned
move through no visible barrier and hits upon his real
object; and that it is, remains—"bestial oblivion"—unknown to him. Why "only then"?—because his pursuit
of the King's guilt is a means to another end, and now
the certainty of it justifies him, it exculpates his own.
The overt conflict with the King is worked out over a

covert conflict in himself, between his father's call to duty and his own desire. The precise nature of that desire may vary with the beholder's eye, but the structure cannot be denied, its object is his mother.

And it is the King at prayer who, a moment earlier, speaks most succinctly for Hamlet's dividedness:

> like a man to double business bound,
> I stand in pause where I should first begin,
> And both neglect.

The true barrier between Hamlet and revenge is lack of self-knowledge of his inner contradiction; move, barrier, object, all have been surrogates.

The structure is thus an image of what three centuries later we will call the unconscious—a piece of Hamlet's, if it is deliberate, a piece of Shakespeare's if not—and indeed the exposition in its entirety is an invitation into the psyche. Its first move, telling Hamlet of the ghost, breaks the surface of a present resignation; its second, seeking the ghost, is Hamlet's journey to know the underworld of the past; its third, his promise of revenge, is a vow to confront the enemy in the future. But which enemy?—a quest for "truth," the action is a descent into the realm of intrapsychic conflict, and the character and play live for us on a level of conflictual depth not equalled in literature. The writing is also talented.

The struggle with the King must of course be consummated, and the third-act pivot creates a serious problem for the subsequent working-out; we shall come to it in due time. First we must re-examine these three acts from another angle.

17. *Consecutivity*

It is self-evident that, in a structure we are to perceive in time, consecutivity is a primary dimension; the order in which we experience its units itself affects our perception of them. In drama the sequences of the moves, a second leading from a first and to a third, is what makes the characters persuasive and their interplay intelligible. In cutting for performance, two-thirds of the text of these plays may be omitted and all run smoothly; omit one move, or scramble three, and the play is derailed. Done deliberately, this makes for what we call a thriller, which gives us consequences before causes, but we are promised restitution later. It is the technique used, deliberately, with the enigma of the King's guilt in the first three acts. Done not deliberately, it is the commonest fault in amateur playmaking, issuing in false leads and meaningless enigmas.

Much of what remains enigmatic in Hamlet's character is born of a mishap with the text, and a resultant inconsecutivity of his moves.

The text I quote from, familiar to all, was first pub-

lished in 1604. Until a hundred and fifty years ago it was
the earliest; then a copy of a 1603 printing was discovered, and a debate of scholars ensued. Undeniably the
same play, its text is half as long, is miserable with errors,
and butchers the poetry the world has by heart. Here as
a sample is Hamlet's best-known soliloquy—

To be, or not to be, I there's the point,
To Die, to sleepe, is that all? I all:
No, to sleepe, to dreame, I mary there it goes,
For in that dream of death, when wee awake,
And borne before an everlasting Judge,
From whence no passenger ever return'd,
The undiscovered country, at whose sight
The happy smile, and the accursed damn'd.
But for this, the joyfull hope of this,
Who'ld beare the scornes and flattery of the world,
Scorned by the right rich, the rich curssed of the poore?
The widow being oppressed, the orphan wrong'd,
The taste of hunger, or a tirants raigne,
And thousand more calamities besides,
To grunte and sweate under this weary life,
When that he may his full Quietus make,
With a bare bodkin, who would this indure,
But for a hope of something after death?
Which pulses the brain, and doth confound the sence,
Which makes us rather beare those evilles we have,
That flie to others that we know not of.
I that, O this conscience makes cowardes of us all,
Lady in thy orizons, be all my sinnes remembred—

and, as one editor said, who wants to go back to that?
The debate was only between two views of this primitive variant: one, it is an early version by Shakespeare in
his twenties, which he reworked in the later years of his
mastery; the other, it is a pirated version, jotted down in

performances and rushed into print, to cash in on a hit play. I like the second view, for reasons which will emerge, and am convinced the tin ear manifest in 1603 never—not one year earlier nor ten—grew on our poet's head.

Our 1604 text announced itself as "newly imprinted and enlarged to almost as much again as it was, according to the true and perfect copy"; it so obviously is, that the 1603 printing remains a scholars' curiosity. Here then we will work again from the standard text, and attempt to untangle the other enigmas lurking in it. But we shall be left afterwards—like the bank that advises us to "consolidate" our small debts—with a larger enigma, to which there is no answer.

The inexorable rise of the first act—the happening, the marshalling of the moves, the catching-up of inert materials by them—we need not comment on again; we are clearly in the hands of a master. We then enter the second act, and are in the hands of an idiot genius who has forgotten half of what he knows.

At the first-act curtain he has given us a Hamlet transfigured by the ghost's tale—

> Remember thee!
> Ay, thou poor ghost, while memory holds a seat
> In this distracted globe. Remember thee!
> Yea, from the table of my memory
> I'll wipe away all trivial fond records—

and fixing upon his life's promise to "set it right!" Surely from such a springboard we shall next meet him taking off? girding himself to "act"? at least *thinking* of our subject? No, he is reading a book.

POLONIUS   How does my good Lord Hamlet?
HAMLET   Well, God-a-mercy.
POLONIUS   Do you know me, my lord?
HAMLET   Excellent well; you are a fishmonger.
POLONIUS   Not I, my lord.
HAMLET   Then I would you were so honest a man.
POLONIUS   Honest, my lord!
HAMLET   Ay, sir; to be honest, as this world goes, is to be one man picked out of ten thousand.
POLONIUS   That's very true, my lord.

And so on. In their conversation Hamlet shows no recollection of the night's events on the parapet, is unprovokedly mocking to Polonius, alludes to Ophelia for no reason, and concludes, "These tedious old fools!"—which is its keynote as usually acted for farcical values, others being undetectable. What is our hero up to, what is his *move?*—nothing; he is standing around.

Enter Rosencrantz and Guildenstern, and in a fine conversation we hear more of Hamlet's darker view—

. . . and yet, to me, what is this quintessence of dust? man delights not me; no, nor woman neither—

but it is retrogressive, we had the world as "unweeded garden" three scenes before the ghost gave him a mission; and his suspicion of his friends—"Were you not sent for?"—is again unprovoked. There is more mocking of Polonius about his daughter, a perseverant meandering which suggests Hamlet is truly disoriented, and the players arrive. Shop-talk about the theatre follows, the actor does his Hecuba bit, and they are sent to their quarters; *now* Hamlet manages to remember the play he was in a full act ago—

HAMLET . . . . old friend; can you play *The Murder of Gonzago?*

PLAYER Ay, my lord.

HAMLET We'll ha't tomorrow night. You could, for a need, study a speech of some dozen or sixteen lines, which I would set down and insert in 't, could you not?—

and we are at the end of the second act. If we are scoring acts like rounds, this one is the King's; throughout it Hamlet has been as baffling a do-nothing as his posthumous reputation promises.

But he is back in the drama—has a plan, a move—and leaves us at act's end with a new rallying cry, also unforgettable:

> The play's the thing
> Wherein I'll catch the conscience of the king.

Surely from such a springboard we shall meet him in the third act taking off, etc.? No, he is next seen talking to himself.

> To be, or not to be: that is the question:
> Whether 'tis nobler in the mind to suffer
> The slings and arrows of outrageous fortune
> Or to take arms—

What?—in the fever of laying a trap for the King he is debating is life worth living? and reproaching himself as

> sicklied o'er with the pale cast of thought,
> And enterprises of great pitch and moment
> With this regard their currents turn awry

precisely when he is in the full rush of one? Two noted actors, meeting after separate disappointments in the role, agreed it was ungraspable; of course it is, the char-

142

acter cannot remember from scene to scene what he is doing.

It is interrupted, whatever it is, by Ophelia with her eavesdroppers in the wings:

> OPHELIA   Good my lord,
> How does your honour for this many a day?
> HAMLET   I humbly thank you: well, well, well.

It is hardly the tone of a man about to topple a king, nor is

> What should such fellows as I do crawling between heaven and earth?

And when he suspects the eavesdroppers—we must infer this, no stage directions, but in the 1603 text Ophelia exclaims, "Great God of heaven, what a quick change is this?"—and rants at her wantonness, for the King's ear, and shouts

> those that are married already, all but one, shall live

it is a rage of impotence, floundering in search of a way; he has forgotten his trap of the play just as earlier he forgot the murder.

It is sprung, nevertheless, and he by-passes the King to take up with his mother the question of her sexual life. It is a brilliant encounter. Is it a scene?—it begins as one, move and object meet, but at its end he is telling her no more than at its beginning, neither has been altered; someone, hero or playwright, has forgotten the issue of the Queen's complicity. Thus no new move is born of the encounter; it is half a scene, and leaves the play stuck.

The genuine paradox in Hamlet, which is seen structurally in the King's serving as surrogate for the Queen, is complex enough for one play. Add to it now the play-wright's change of heart in first picking up the device of feigned madness from his source, and then dropping it half-used; the confusion, if not the complexity, grows. Add to this doubt of his sanity a text in which the character cannot remember his own course of action, with erratic back-trackings, and he becomes truly not possible to follow. And since we cannot follow, we take it for profundity.

In my youth a Hollywood version of *The Taming of the Shrew* gave script-credit to "William Shakespeare, additional dialogue by Sam Cohen"; without going quite that far, can we not lend a hand to this poor writer? Let us relocate one great chunk of his own words. We will lift out of the third act both the soliloquy "To be or not to be" and its companion scene with Ophelia and eavesdroppers; we will advance them into the second act, as Hamlet's first appearance therein. What happens to the character in the curve of the three acts?

Now from the springboard of the first we see Hamlet next, in the celebrated soliloquy, probing his situation in almost an unbroken thought—

> O cursed spite,
> That ever I was born to set it right!
>
> To be, or not to be: that is the question:
> Whether 'tis nobler in the mind—

debating not suicide, but sufferance versus resistance, and cautioning himself against the dangers of thought. It is not gratuitous philosophy; it is a clearing of the decks for action, its nature as yet unknown to him. Enter

Ophelia with her spies, and now his self-doubting tone—
is the ghost "honest" or the voice of his own ambition to
be king?—

Get thee to a nunnery: why wouldst thou be a breeder of
sinners? I am myself indifferent honest; but yet I could ac-
cuse me of such things that it were better my mother had
not borne me: I am very proud, revengeful, ambitious. . . .
Where's your father?

is as appropriate as his immediate rage crying out
obliquely on both Queen and King; spied on, he is most
vulnerable now, casting about for his own means of attack.

We pick up the standard text here, with Polonius
emerging and innocently accosting Hamlet—

> POLONIUS   Do you know me, my lord?
> HAMLET   Excellent well; you are a fishmonger—

—panderer? fishing for secrets?—and Hamlet's cruelty to
him in every line

I would you were so honest a man—

Have you a daughter? . . . . Let her not walk i' the sun:
conception is a blessing; but not as your daughter may conceive—

. . . . the satirical rogue says here that old men have grey
beards, that their faces are wrinkled, their eyes purging
thick amber and plum-tree gum, and that they have a plen-
tiful lack of wit—

now comes directly out of the lethal eavesdropping:

> POLONIUS   I will most humbly take my leave of you.
> HAMLET   You cannot, sir, take from me any thing that I

145

will more willingly part withal: except my life, except my life, except my life.

It is not farce, a clever young man having fun with a dotard; he is playing with the enemy for life and death.

> POLONIUS   Will you walk out of the air, my lord?
> HAMLET   Into my grave?

And now he has a precedent to suspect his old school-mates are turning up also as spies, and immediate reason to greet them with

HAMLET   Denmark's a prison.
ROSENCRANTZ   Then is the world one.
HAMLET   A goodly one; in which there are many confines, wards, and dungeons, Denmark being one o' the worst—

as the dangers close in on him; he is not standing around, he is walking among snakes. Polonius returns to announce the players, and after a last allusion to his scheming—

HAMLET   O Jephthah, judge of Israel, what a treasure hadst thou! . . . .
POLONIUS   (*aside*)   Still on my daughter.
HAMLET   Am I not i' the right, old Jephthah?—

Hamlet sees the players as his move, and seizes upon it; with the eavesdropping moved to its outset, the entire act has been charged as preparation for this choice.

More, the soliloquy and eavesdropping scene are no longer roadblocks to the character's thrust in the third act. From the springboard of the second we see him next instructing the players in almost an unbroken thought—

the play's the thing
Wherein I'll catch the conscience of the king.

Speak the speech, I pray you, as I pronounced it to you,
trippingly on the tongue—

crisp with his business; his alerting of Horatio—

> There is a play tonight before the king;
> One scene of it comes near the circumstance
> Which I have told thee of my father's death:
> I prithee, when thou seest that act—

and the taut pitch of his sallies with the King and
Ophelia—

> KING   Is there no offence in 't?
> HAMLET   No, no, they do but jest, poison in jest; no offence
> i' the world.
> KING   What do you call the play?
> HAMLET   *The Mousetrap.* . . .
> OPHELIA   You are keen, my lord, you are keen.
> HAMLET   It would cost you a groaning to take off my edge—

are all of a piece off that springboard; not once now
does he fall back into the soul-searching so right between
mission and means in the second act, but in the third dif-
fusive of the play's climb to its pivot.

Finally, in the Queen's bedchamber, we must call in
Sam for a few words of new dialogue—

> QUEEN   But as I have a soul, I swear by heaven
> I never knew of this most horrid murder.
> HAMLET   And mother, but assist me in revenge,
> And in his death your infamy shall die.
> QUEEN   I will conceal, consent, and do my best
> What stratagem soe'er thou shalt devise—

to complete the scene with the promise of a new move; and we are done.

It is a beautiful line, from Hamlet's first moment in the play on, vibrant as a bowstring for three acts; the character is always followable, retains every vacillation bred of his inner contradiction, and is clean of nonsensical accruals from a text of mangled consecutivity; and it fits with everything we have seen of the playwright's habit of mind in these pages.

It is how he first wrote it.

I venture to say so—it is not a new view—because I have only duplicated here the layout of the 1603 version, and added dialogue from it. What happened between the 1603 and 1604 printings is part of the larger enigma of Shakespeare's attitude to his work. We do not know that he ever proofread or laid eyes upon one word of his plays in print; we know only that half of them—eighteen, including *The Tempest, Measure for Measure, Twelfth Night, Julius Caesar, Coriolanus, Antony and Cleopatra, As You Like It, The Taming of the Shrew, The Comedy of Errors, The Winter's Tale, Macbeth*—would have been lost to us forever if his colleagues had not collected them for publication seven years after his death. It may be that the greatest body of theatre literature in modern history was created by an actor-businessman indifferent to its fate.

18. *Unfinished Business*

In a number of these plays—chosen almost at random, others would do as well—we have followed the working-out in its rise move by move. This part of the playwright's game is, as we saw, the course his master move takes in its struggle around the barrier to get at the master object; it has called into being everything else in the play, and crystallized its theme in the third-act pivot. From this pivot, like a continental divide, the working-out plunges down towards that moveless sea we call the end.

What remains?

The form we have drawn from the many workings-out of these plays is an abstraction. The move of course does seek its object. But the single-plot thrust in *Hamlet* towards an object which conceals another is different from that in *Macbeth* towards one object given from the first; the use in *Macbeth* of successive surrogates for the antagonist is different from their use for the surprise move in *The Merchant of Venice*; the double-plotting which in *The Merchant of Venice* moves a completed narrative against a drama as object is different from that which in *Lear* interfits the incomplete moves and objects of two half-dramas. The form is an ideal, each play deviates from it uniquely, and in its uniqueness is its meaning.

So too with the working-out in its final phase. Here the playwright's task is to gather all the open questions of the preceding acts into the closure of answer; the hugest is of course that of the rendezvous of master move and object. If the exposition is the most tangled stretch of the play, its plunge is the most direct, and offers the fewest options: the questions contain the answer. But each wrap-up is unique too, and in arriving at it the playwright must not fail his great occasion, the rendezvous which crowns all; it should be unforgettable.

It seldom is not, in the tragedies. Little remains to be debated by the antagonists in this moment, but who can forget the scenes?—Juliet awakening in her tomb to the horror of Romeo's corpse, Othello killing Desdemona in their bed, Hamlet waging the duel which becomes a massacre, Lear heartbroken with the slain Cordelia in his arms? Their deaths are as indelible as those of our relatives.

In the comedies, all is more lax, including the close. No one forgets Portia in her legal robes at the trial, but that comes a full act before the end; and which of my readers can recall offhand the decisive encounter in *The Tempest*?

Let us turn to the plunge in each, beginning with this charming magic-show, the most deviant play of all.

19. *The Plunge, Comic*

The Tempest is seen by a variety of scholars as the author's last will and testament, one of the most perfect of his plays, and a personal farewell to his dear public; others think it among the earliest. The dating of the plays is a lifework for moles, and has driven a few crazy. We shall look only at structure; the flavor of the writing is late, the structure short-circuits everything the playwright has led us to expect.

Its opening storm, and Prospero's exegesis of it to Miranda, we noted earlier; his magic has brought to the island a shipful of nobles, including his brother Antonio who twelve years back banished him—yes, another—to usurp his dukedom. The second scene gives us his sprite Ariel, his monster Caliban, and a young prince he makes prisoner, Ferdinand, who talks with the easy beauty characteristic of the play:

> Sitting on a bank,
> Weeping again the king my father's wreck,
> This music crept by me upon the waters,

> Allaying both their fury and my passion
> With its sweet air. . . .

Miranda and this prince fall in love, Prospero murmuring

> As my soul prompts it. . . . At the first sight
> They have changed eyes.

There are now two promises, Prospero's unknown purpose with Antonio and a love story; the energy is mild.

The second act is also in two scenes. The first acquaints us with the nobles around the King of Naples; and the wicked Antonio works at sinuous length upon the King's brother—yes, another—to kill him in his sleep.

SEBASTIAN   I remember
  You did supplant your brother Prospero.
ANTONIO   True:
  And look how well my garments sit upon me;
  Much feater than before: my brother's servants
  Were then my fellows; now they are my men.
SEBASTIAN   But for your conscience.
ANTONIO   Ay, sir; where lies that? . . . . Here lies your
     brother,
  No better than the earth he lies upon,
  If he were that which now he's like, that's dead;
  Whom I, with this obedient steel, three inches of it,
  Can lay to bed for ever. . . .
SEBASTIAN   Thy case, dear friend,
  Shall be my precedent; as thou got'st Milan,
  I'll come by Naples. Draw thy sword . . .
  And I the king shall love thee.
ANTONIO   Draw together.

But Ariel flies in to rouse the King in time; the third promise is of a later attempt.

The second scene gives us the lower-class, Caliban

and a jester and a butler Stephano with a bottle of wine; after some drunken horseplay—I am skipping the jokes, most of them still funny—Caliban adopts the butler as his god, who announces that

the king and all our company else being drowned, we will inherit here,

and Caliban leads them off on a tour of the isle, chanting:

>'Ban, 'Ban, Cacaliban
>Has a new master: get a new man.

His revolt is a fourth promise.

The third act furthers two of these promises, alludes to the third, and divulges the content of Prospero's purpose, the master move. Its first scene picks up the love story— the captive Ferdinand is bearing a log, Miranda comes, and Prospero eavesdrops:

MIRANDA   Alas, now, pray you,
   Work not so hard. . . .
   Pray, set it down, and rest you: when this burns,
   'Twill weep for having wearied you. . . .
FERDINAND   O most dear mistress,
   The sun will set before I shall discharge
   What I must strive to do.
MIRANDA   If you'll sit down,
   I'll bear your logs the while. . . .
PROSPERO (*aside*)   Poor worm, thou art infected!

The lovers exchange vows, the scene ends. The second picks up Caliban and his drunken friends, with Ariel invisible, as they plot to kill Prospero:

CALIBAN   I say, by sorcery he got this isle;
   From me he got it. If thy greatness will

Revenge it on him. . . .
Thou shalt be lord of it, and I'll serve thee.

STEPHANO How now shall this be encompassed? Canst thou
bring me to the party?

CALIBAN Yea, yea, my lord: I'll yield him thee asleep,
Where thou mayst knock a nail into his head. . . .
And that most deeply to consider is
The beauty of his daughter; he himself
Calls her a nonpareil. . . .

STEPHANO Is it so brave a lass?

CALIBAN Ay, lord; she will become thy bed, I warrant,
And bring thee forth brave brood.

STEPHANO Monster, I will kill this man: his daughter and I
will be king and queen. . . .

CALIBAN Within this half hour will he be asleep:
Wilt thou destroy him then?

STEPHANO Ay, on mine honour.

ARIEL (*aside*) This will I tell my master.

And Ariel leads them astray with piping. The third scene
picks up the nobles, following the King in search of his
son Ferdinand, thought drowned; the wicked brothers
speak aside.

ANTONIO Do not, for one repulse, forego the purpose
That you resolved to effect.

SEBASTIAN   The next advantage
Will we take thoroughly.

ANTONIO   Let it be tonight.

Now Prospero and his spirits set before these starvelings
the illusion of a sumptuous banquet; alas, when they
move to eat, it vanishes—"with a quaint device"—in
thunder and lightning. Ariel in the form of a harpy ad-
dresses Antonio, Sebastian, and the King:

You are three men of sin. . . .
From Milan did supplant good Prospero;
Exposed unto the sea, which hath requit it,
Him and his innocent child: for which foul deed
The powers, delaying, not forgetting, have
Incensed the seas and shores, yea, all the creatures,
Against your peace. . . . whose wraths to guard you
    from,—
Which here, in this most desolate isle, else falls
Upon your heads,—is nothing but heart-sorrow
And a clear life ensuing.

So their penitence is what Prospero requires—and gets,
the King is staggered:

> O, it is monstrous, monstrous!
> Methought the billows spoke, and told me of it;
> The winds did sing it to me; and the thunder,
> That deep and dreadful organ-pipe, pronounced
> The name of Prosper: it did bass my trespass.
> Therefore my son i' th' ooze is bedded; and
> I'll . . . . with him there lie mudded.

This is the third-act pivot, and its theme is clear: the
feast of evil is illusory. But this is symbol and magic, not
human work of will, it is the antithesis of drama. The de-
ployment of the familiar structure is odd. Most of the
exposition has been in flat do-you-remember exchanges
of facts known to all, empty of future; when Prospero
with a pass puts Ferdinand in bondage, he informs us it
is only pretense—not even Rosalind's costume stands between these lovers; we have one genuine scene in Antonio's inciting of Sebastian, and Ariel, both in forestall-
ing that murder—

    My master through his art foresees the danger—

and in warning Prospero of the other, cancels out all suspense. Nowhere is there a barrier. We are in a realm of sorcery too facile for drama, and surely the playwright knows it?—every touch is a lulling. And his most winsome character, this monster Caliban, a poet from his opening plaint to Prospero—

> When thou camest first,
> Thou strokedst me, and madest much of me; wouldst give
>   me
> Water with berries in't; and teach me how
> To name the bigger light, and how the less,
> That burn by day and night: and then I lov'd thee,
> And show'd thee all the qualities o' th' isle,
> The fresh springs, brine-pits, barren place and fertile:
> Cursed be I that did so! . . . .
> For I am all the subjects that you have,
> Which first was mine own king—

is now, in the middle of his inept revolt, a music-lover too:

> Be not afeared; the isle is full of noises,
> Sounds and sweet airs, that give delight, and hurt not.
> Sometimes a thousand twangling instruments
> Will hum about mine ears. . . . and then, in dreaming,
> The clouds methought would open, and show riches
> Ready to drop upon me; that, when I waked,
> I cried to dream again.

The work is a lyric.

It now turns for its plunge; and there is none. There are only two scenes left, one per act, and the unfinished business is swept hastily under the magic carpet. The promise of the King's murder—"Let it be tonight"—is disposed of simply, night never comes; one scene disposes of the lovers and Caliban, and the other of Prospero's purpose.

In the fourth act he gives Ferdinand his blessing, and apologizes for the log:

> If I have too austerely punish'd you,
> Your compensation makes amends; for I
> Have given you here a third of mine own life,
> Or that for which I live. . . . all thy vexations
> Were but my trials of thy love. . . .

And now—

> I must
> Bestow upon the eyes of this young couple
> Some vanity of mine art: it is my promise,
> And they expect it—

he invokes against all our wishes a formal masque, in rhyme, of classical goddesses and nymphs and reapers, who dance, and sing for the lovers in courtly tongue:

> Ceres, most bounteous lady, thy rich leas
> Of wheat, rye, barley, vetches, oats, and pease;
> Thy turfy mountains, where live nibbling sheep,
> And flat meads thatch'd with stover, them to keep;
> Thy banks with pioned and twilled brims,
> Which spongy April at thy hest betrims. . . .

Ferdinand calls it "a most majestic vision"; it is a fertility rite, and the key to the work. Its poetry is academic straw, but Prospero caps it with the great speech of the play:

> Our revels now are ended. These our actors,
> As I foretold you, were all spirits, and
> Are melted into air, into thin air:
> And, like the baseless fabric of this vision,

> The cloud-capp'd towers, the gorgeous palaces,
> The solemn temples, the great globe itself,
> Yea, all which it inherit, shall dissolve,
> And, like this insubstantial pageant faded,
> Leave not a rack behind. We are such stuff
> As dreams are made on; and our little life
> Is rounded with a sleep.

He has restated the moral of the banquet, *vanitas vanitatum*, and now presents it a third time as comedy; he tells Ariel

> The trumpery in my house, go bring it hither,
> For stale to catch these thieves,

and Ariel hangs on a line a load of "glistering apparel, etc." When Caliban leads his drunken friends in to Prospero's cell, they dive upon these riches:

TRINCULO   O worthy Stephano! look what a wardrobe here is for thee!

CALIBAN   Let it alone, thou fool; it is but trash.

TRINCULO   O, ho monster! we know what belongs to a frippery. O King Stephano!

STEPHANO   Put off that gown, Trinculo; by this hand, I'll have that gown.

TRINCULO   Thy grace shall have it.

CALIBAN   The dropsy drown this fool! what do you mean
To dote thus on such luggage? Let's alone,
And do the murder first.

But they can think only of the loot, and while they are pawing it over Prospero routs them all with spirits as "dogs and hounds, hunting them about."

In the final act he turns to the completion of his purpose, the "heart-sorrow and a clear life ensuing" of the aristocracy; Ariel tells him they are so

> Brimful of sorrow and dismay. . . .
> That if you now beheld them, your affections
> Would become tender.
> PROSPERO   Dost thou think so, spirit?
> ARIEL   Mine would, sir, were I human.
> PROSPERO   And mine shall. . . .
> . . . with my nobler reason 'gainst my fury
> Do I take part: the rarer action is
> In virtue than in vengeance: they being penitent,
> The sole drift of my purpose doth extend
> Not a frown further. . . . I'll break my staff,
> Bury it certain fathoms in the earth,
> And deeper than did ever plummet sound
> I'll drown my book.

The work of his magic is done, all that remains is forgiveness; so the King and his nobles are brought in,
stupefied.

> PROSPERO   Their understanding
> Begins to swell; and the approaching tide
> Will shortly fill the reasonable shore,
> That now lies foul and muddy. . . .
> For you, most wicked sir, whom to call brother
> Would even infect my mouth, I do forgive
> Thy rankest fault—all of them.

And to the King he reveals his lost son Ferdinand, playing chess in a cell with Miranda; she knows only two
men, and so cries out, gazing upon this flock of villains—

> How beauteous mankind is! O brave new world,
> That has such people in 't!
> PROSPERO   'Tis new to thee.

It is a mournful line; but the love of such innocents is all
his answer to the illusion of the world. The play is done.
An old courtier sums up the theme for the peerage—

> set it down
> With gold on lasting pillars: In one voyage
> . . . . Ferdinand . . . . found a wife
> Where he himself was lost, Prospero his dukedom
> In a poor isle, and all of us ourselves
> When no man was his own—

and Stephano in a drunken mix-up for the rabble:

Every man shift for all the rest, and let no man take care for himself; for all is but fortune.

It is the time's thought, the identical message which— seven years after this play saw print—a silenced minister preached to the Puritan fleet running up sail for a brave new world in Massachusetts.

Now what are we to make of this aborted structure, in a work so strangely beautiful, timely, and boring?— the playwright has forgone half his skills for keeping an audience in the theatre. But what if his audience was not in a theatre?

It has been speculated that *The Tempest* was written for the court revels on the occasion of a royal wedding; believe it, and all falls in place. The hymeneal masque, otherwise so unwelcome, now becomes the centerpiece.

> It is my promise,
> And they expect it.

The play of fanciful action surrounding it is itself masque-like; the magic antithetical to drama is perfect for spectacle; the lulling of every threat befits the festive mood. And the audience is captive. What is then surprising is not that the energy is mild, but that the playwright has used the nuptial event to deliver so strong a sermon on the vanity of loveless power, and that to his betters.

So seen, it is a most original hybrid, half play, half masque—if a play, unfulfilled, but if a masque, the greatest ever written.

In a comedy devised for us low theatregoers, *The Merchant of Venice*, we find a real plunge, so headlong it kills both plots in the fourth act; our author is hard put to take us through a fifth.

So he invokes a third plot. One indeed is already exhausted when Bassanio, in no need of Prospero's lesson, ponders the caskets—

> The world is still deceived with ornament.
> . . . . thou meagre lead,
> Which rather threatenest than dost promise aught,
> Thy paleness moves me more than eloquence—

and opens the lid on Portia's portrait.

> PORTIA   You see me, Lord Bassanio, where I stand,
> Such as I am . . . . but now I was the lord
> Of this fair mansion, master of my servants,
> Queen o'er myself; and even now, but now,
> This house, these servants, and this same myself,
> Are yours, my lord: I give them with this ring;
> Which when you part from, lose or give away,
> Let it presage the ruin of your love. . . .
> BASSANIO   Madam, you have bereft me of all words,
> Only—

and he goes on at some length, concluding

> . . . when this ring
> Parts from this finger, then parts life from hence.

161

Antonio's letter now calls Bassanio back to Venice for the trial, and Portia plots to follow secretly with her maid Nerissa; we are at the third-act pivot, except for a scenelet which concludes the act. It is a freak in these plays; featuring Shylock's daughter and her Christian lover, it lacks even a story-point, and only marks time. Why was it written?—perhaps to cover Portia's change of costume. But it is full of jesting talk about Christians and Jews.

The unfinished business now consists of one item, the master promise. Portia is the move, the object is Shylock —or, Antonio's survival—and the barrier between is the pound-of-flesh bond; the coming trial will fulfil this promise and the play. But the third plot has been smuggled in.

The fourth act, opening in "a court of justice," must give us Shylock as immovable object; it does, and more, for now the ideological antithesis implicit in the play breaks to the surface:

DUKE   Shylock, the world thinks, and I think so too,
  That thou but lead'st this fashion of thy malice
  To the last hour of act; and then 'tis thought
  Thou 'lt show thy mercy. . . .
  We all expect a gentle answer, Jew.
SHYLOCK   I have possess'd your Grace of what I purpose;
  And by our holy Sabbath have I sworn
  To have the due and forfeit of my bond:
  If you deny it, let the danger light
  Upon your charter and your city's freedom.

One is the voice of Christian love, the other that of Mosaic law, and both, in human throats, cracking; as Shylock says,

162

affection,
Mistress of passion, sways it to the mood
Of what it likes or loathes.

The arguments rise, and Shylock by no means has the
worst of it.

SHYLOCK   What if my house be troubled with a rat,
   And I be pleased to give ten thousand ducats
   To have it baned? . . . .
BASSANIO   This is no answer, thou unfeeling man. . . .
SHYLOCK   I am not bound to please thee with my answer.
BASSANIO   Do all men kill the things they do not love? . . . .
SHYLOCK   What, wouldst thou have a serpent sting thee
   twice?
ANTONIO   I pray you, think you question with the Jew:
   You may as well go stand upon the beach,
   And bid the main flood bate. . . .
   As seek to soften that—than which what's harder?—
   His Jewish heart. . . .
DUKE   How shalt thou hope for mercy, rendering
   none? . . . .
SHYLOCK   You have among you many a purchased slave. . . .
   You use in abject and in slavish parts,
   Because you bought them: shall I say to you,
   Let them be free, marry them to your heirs?
   Why sweat they under burthens?

It is into this debate of values that Portia comes, disguised in legal robes, and her first question is

   Which is the merchant here, and which the Jew?

not unlike Lear's

change places: and, handy-dandy, which is the justice,
which the thief?

She is present to save Antonio and uphold the sanctity of law; she states both the dilemma—

PORTIA   Is your name Shylock?
SHYLOCK   Shylock is my name.
PORTIA   Of a strange nature is the suit you follow;
   Yet in such a rule that the Venetian law
   Cannot impugn you as you do proceed.
   You stand within his danger, do you not?
ANTONIO   Ay, so he says.
PORTIA   Do you confess the bond?
ANTONIO   I do—

and the way out:

     PORTIA   Then must the Jew be merciful.

It gives birth to the great speech of *this* play—

   SHYLOCK   On what compulsion must I? tell me that.
   PORTIA   The quality of mercy is not strain'd,
     It droppeth as the gentle rain from heaven
     Upon the place beneath: it is twice blest;
     It blesseth him that gives, and him that takes:
     'Tis mightiest in the mightiest: it becomes
     The throned monarch better than his crown. . . .
     And earthly power doth then show likest God's
     When mercy seasons justice. Therefore, Jew,
     Though justice be thy plea, consider this,
     That, in the course of justice, none of us
     Should see salvation—

and this indeed is Nazarene doctrine at its very heart, spoken in an era convulsed by the Lutheran dichotomy of works and grace. It falls upon deaf ears, not for the first time—

     SHYLOCK   I crave the law—

164

and Portia now weighs in the balance a portion of law—

> BASSANIO   I beseech you,
>   Wrest once the law to your authority:
>   To do a great right, do a little wrong,
>   And curb this cruel devil of his will.
> PORTIA   It must not be; there is no power in Venice
>   Can alter a decree established:
>   'Twill be recorded for a precedent,
>   And many an error, by the same example,
>   Will rush into the state: it cannot be—

and a portion of mercy—

> PORTIA   Shylock, there's thrice thy money offer'd thee.
> SHYLOCK   An oath, an oath. I have an oath in heaven—

and of law—

> PORTIA   This bond is forfeit;
>   And lawfully by this the Jew may claim
>   A pound of flesh, to be by him cut off
>   Nearest the merchant's heart—

and of mercy—

> PORTIA   Be merciful:
>   Take thrice thy money; bid me tear the bond. . . .
> SHYLOCK   Proceed to judgement; by my soul I swear
>   There is no power in the tongue of man
>   To alter me—

and of law—

> ANTONIO   Most heartily I do beseech the court
>   To give the judgement.
> PORTIA   Why then, thus it is:
>   You must prepare your bosom for his knife.
> SHYLOCK   O noble judge!—

165

and of mercy—

PORTIA   Have by some surgeon, Shylock, on your charge,
   To stop his wounds, lest he do bleed to death.
SHYLOCK   Is it so nominated in the bond?
PORTIA   It is not so express'd: but what of that?
   'Twere good you do so much for charity.
SHYLOCK   I cannot find it; 'tis not in the bond—

until she invites Antonio's last word. It is the climactic
moment, but interrupted by some wry by-play between
the disguised ladies and their husbands:

BASSANIO   Antonio, I am married to a wife
   Which is as dear to me as life itself;
   But life itself, my wife, and all the world,
   Are not with me esteem'd above thy life. . . .
PORTIA   Your wife would give you little thanks for that,
   If she were by. . . .
GRATIANO   I have a wife, whom, I protest, I love:
   I would she were in heaven, so she could
   Entreat some power to change this currish Jew.
NERISSA   'Tis well you offer it behind her back;
   The wish would make else an unquiet house.
SHYLOCK   These be the Christian husbands. I have a daugh-
      ter;
   Would any of the stock of Barrabas
   Had been her husband rather than a Christian!

Why at this tense moment?—because Portia's next move
will end the double plot, and the playwright is seeding
a fifth act. Here is the move:

PORTIA   A pound of that same merchant's flesh is thine:
   The court awards it, and the law doth give it.
SHYLOCK   Most rightful judge!
PORTIA   And you must cut this flesh off his breast:
   The law allows it, and the court awards it.

166

SHYLOCK   Most learned judge! A sentence! Come, prepare!
PORTIA   Tarry a little; there is something else.
  This bond doth give thee here no jot of blood.

It is a legal quibble, the whole play turns on it, and we
may find it more forgivable if we view this dénouement
as a savaging of all human justice; laws now fall on Shylock's head like boulders.

> PORTIA   If thou dost shed
>   One drop of Christian blood, thy lands and goods
>   Are, by the laws of Venice, confiscate
>   Unto the state. . . .
> SHYLOCK   Is that the law? . . .
> PORTIA   Thou shalt have justice, more than thou
>   desirest. . . .
> SHYLOCK   I take this offer, then; pay the bond thrice,
>   And let the Christian go.
> BASSANIO   Here is the money.

But Portia will have only law now—

> PORTIA   He shall have nothing but the penalty.
>   . . . . nor cut thou less nor more
>   But just a pound of flesh. . . . if the scale do turn
>   But in the estimation of a hair,
>   Thou diest and all thy goods are confiscate. . . .
> SHYLOCK   Give me my principal, and let me go.
> BASSANIO   I have it ready for thee. . . .
> PORTIA   He shall have merely justice and his bond. . . .
> SHYLOCK   Why, then the devil give him good of it!
>   I'll stay no longer question.
> PORTIA   Tarry, Jew:
>   The law hath yet another hold on you.
>   It is enacted in the laws of Venice,
>   If it be proved against an alien

That by direct or indirect attempts
He seek the life of any citizen,
. . . . the offender's life lies in the mercy
Of the Duke only. . . .
Down, therefore, and beg mercy of the Duke—

and so drives Shylock to mercy as recipient; the Duke shows "the difference of our spirits" by pardoning his life and stripping him of all his wealth.

SHYLOCK   Nay, take my life and all; pardon not that:
You take my house, when you do take the prop
That doth sustain my house. . . .
PORTIA   What mercy can you render him, Antonio?
GRATIANO   A halter gratis. . . .

But Antonio gives him back half the fine, and Shylock totters off with half a life too; he is under sentence to "presently become a Christian."

The play is done, two-thirds into the fourth act. Except—

A promise has been born, Portia and her maid must come out from their legal robes; it could be worked in a jiffy here. But the author wants a fifth act in a playful mood. So of a minor necessity he makes an extended game, to span another two scenes, by calling in the third plot; it is a risky process, additive, not concentric, and any addendum weakens the original structure.

BASSANIO   Take some remembrance of us, as a tribute,
Not as a fee. . . .
PORTIA   You press me far. . . .
And, for your love, I'll take this ring from you:
Do not draw back your hand. . . .
BASSANIO   This ring, good sir, alas, it is a trifle! . . . .
PORTIA   I will have nothing else but only this. . . .

BASSANIO   There's more depends on this than on the
  value. . . .
PORTIA   I see, sir, you are liberal in offers:
  You taught me first to beg. . . .
BASSANIO   Good sir, this ring was given me by my wife. . . .
PORTIA   That 'scuse serves many men to save their gifts.

And she leaves; but he sends it after her, by Gratiano.
Whose wife Nerissa, in the next scene, gets a like ring
back from him. Portia then announces,

> We'll away tonight,
> And be a day before our husbands home,

and a fifth act now is necessary; it is a playlet in itself,
with move, barrier, object.

   In one scene, it takes us back to the ecumenical pair
in Portia's garden, Shylock's daughter and her Christian;
waiting—while Portia "doth stray about by holy crosses,"
no accident—they again summon the music which un-
derscores the love story. Shylock has called it "the sound
of shallow foppery," but they equate it with the peace
that passes understanding:

> Here will we sit, and let the sounds of music
> Creep in our ears: soft stillness and the night
> Become the touches of sweet harmony.
> . . . . Look how the floor of heaven
> Is thick inlaid with patines of bright gold:
> There's not the smallest orb which thou behold'st
> But in his motion like an angel sings,
> Still quiring to the young-eyed cherubins;
> Such harmony is in immortal souls;
> But whilst this muddy vesture of decay
> Doth grossly close it in, we cannot hear it. . . .
> The man that hath no music in himself,

Nor is not moved with concord of sweet sounds,
Is fit for treasons, stratagems and spoils. . . .
Let no such man be trusted. Mark the music.

Enter Portia and Nerissa, on a note echoing the former
plot—

PORTIA   That light we see is burning in my hall.
How far that little candle throws his beams!
So shines a good deed in a naughty world—

and they are soon followed by their menfolk. Gratiano
and Nerissa pick up the new plot:

GRATIANO   I swear you do me wrong;
In faith, I gave it to the judge's clerk:
Would he were gelt that had it. . . .
PORTIA   A quarrel, ho, already! what's the matter?
GRATIANO   About a hoop of gold, a paltry ring
That she did give me. . . .
NERISSA   Gave it a judge's clerk! no, God's my judge,
The clerk will ne'er wear hair on 's face that had it.
GRATIANO   He will, and if he live to be a man.
NERISSA   Ay, if a woman live to be a man.

It is—all mock drama—Portia's move; the "barrier" is
Bassanio's ignorance of her escapade; the object is an
amiable ridiculing of men by women, as is the play itself.

PORTIA   I gave my love a ring, and made him swear
Never to part with it; and here he stands;
I dare be sworn for him he would not leave it
Nor pluck it from his finger, for the wealth
That the world masters. . . .
BASSANIO (*aside*)   Why, I were best to cut my left hand off,
And swear I lost the ring defending it.
GRATIANO   My Lord Bassanio gave his ring away
Unto the judge that begg'd it. . . .
PORTIA   What ring gave you, my lord?

170

The language itself is brought skipping into this game—

BASSANIO   Sweet Portia,
   If you did know to whom I gave the ring,
   If you did know for whom I gave the ring,
   And would conceive for what I gave the ring,
   And how unwillingly I left the ring,
   When nought would be accepted but the ring,
   You would abate the strength of your displeasure.
PORTIA   If you had known the virtue of the ring,
   Or half her worthiness that gave the ring,
   Or your own honour to contain the ring,
   You would not then have parted with the ring. . . .
   I'll die for 't but some woman had the ring.
BASSANIO   No, by my honour. . . .
   No woman had it, but a civil doctor—

and the ladies toy with the onerous side of love's coin,
fidelity.

PORTIA   Let not that doctor e'er come near my house. . . .
   I will become as liberal as you;
   I'll not deny him any thing I have. . . .
   I'll have that doctor for my bedfellow.
NERISSA   And I his clerk. . . .
BASSANIO   I swear to thee, even by thine own fair eyes,
   Wherein I see myself—
PORTIA   Mark you but that! . . . .
   In each eye, one; swear by your double self,
   And there's an oath of credit. . . .
BASSANIO   Pardon this fault, and by my soul I swear
   I never more will break an oath with thee.

Which is all Portia wants to hear.

PORTIA   Give him this,
   And bid him keep it better than the other. . . .
BASSANIO   By heaven, it is the same I gave the doctor!

PORTIA   I had it of him: pardon me, Bassanio;
   For, by this ring, the doctor lay with me.
NERISSA   And pardon me, my gentle Gratiano;
   For that same scrubbed boy, the doctor's clerk,
   In lieu of this last night did lie with me.
GRATIANO   Why, this is like the mending of highways
   In summer, where the ways are fair enough:
   What, are we cuckolds?

Now we see the function of this fifth act; it is a coda whose teasing not only lifts us from the sombreness of Shylock's trial, but reconsiders the basic movement of a comedy in which all giving—from Portia's money to her wisdom in a new ethic—flows from women; this act is their revenge. That savored, Portia dissolves the mock barrier with letters which explain all, even that Antonio's "argosies are richly come to harbour"—

ANTONIO   Sweet lady, you have given me life and living—

and the play is done, for a second time.

20. *Aside*

But how do we know?—it takes no thinking, the instant a play is done we feel it on our skins, like a heat lamp gone off; we are in at a death, a qualitative change. Something has happened in its innards, what is it?

We feel it even in the masque-structure of *The Tempest*. Its promise to us, from the second scene on, is a settling of Prospero's account with his enemies; smaller promises complicate the movement until, in the last scene, he forgives them all. Now the master move and object have met, and each is altered. The enemies are penitent—Antonio utters not a word, but during the play the King as surrogate has been sidled into his place, and says

> Thy dukedom I resign, and do entreat
> Thou pardon me my wrongs—

and can offer no further opposition; Prospero's move has been exhausted, and he can only

> retire me to my Milan, where
> Every third thought shall be my grave.

173

And the barrier?—there has been no barrier, and that is why this frictionless encounter is so forgettable, no heat has been generated. But no further business, either, the movement has stopped.

In *The Merchant of Venice* it stops twice. First, the trial has brought the master move and object face to face, across the barrier, and each in the encounter is altered. It reduces Shylock, in the pound-of-flesh drama, from avenger to victim—

> PORTIA   Art thou contented, Jew? what dost thou say?
> SHYLOCK   I am content.
> PORTIA   Clerk, draw a deed of gift.
> SHYLOCK   I pray you, give me leave to go from hence;
>   I am not well—

and he leaves the play, broken; the move of the love-story against him, in Portia's person—

> PORTIA   He is well paid that is well satisfied;
>   And I, delivering you, am satisfied—

is emptied of all its potential. The barrier itself, the bond, has become the bridge between the two stories, and in their encounter is liquidated. We are at an end; and only a third story, begun earlier, carries us past it. Froth as this is, it brings us again to a meeting of move and object, and when Portia gives back the ring—

> BASSANIO   Sweet doctor, you shall be my bedfellow:
>   When I am absent, then lie with my wife.
> PORTIA   . . . . Let us go in—

the barrier is gone; the movement thus comes to its second stop.

Yet the third plot has renewed it once, could not a

fourth renew it again?—of course, if seeded earlier. Shylock could found a political party to reform the laws of Venice.

We have only half an answer; let us change genres.

21. *The Moveless Sea*

Romeo and Juliet is the first of the great tragedies; published when its author was thirty-three, written
perhaps in his late twenties, it moves on a flood of youth-
ful energies, is prodigal with theatrical event and verbal
artifice, and shipwrecks its lovers on the winds of chance.
Structurally, it is tragedy by fiat, that is, not yet clear of
comedy.

Its opening act gives us, first, the families in a street
duel, and the Prince's decree of death to the next who
breaks the peace, and Romeo melancholy for lack of
love; and then Paris, suing for Juliet's hand of her father,
and invitations to a ball at her house, and Romeo's decision to attend it; and Juliet, with her mother urging her
to marry Paris; and Romeo with his friends, masked for
the ball, although

> my mind misgives
> Some consequence, yet hanging in the stars,
> Shall bitterly begin his fearful date
> With this night's revels,

and then the ball itself, with his first glimpse of Juliet—

> O, she doth teach the torches to burn bright!
> It seems she hangs upon the cheek of night
> Like a rich jewel in an Ethiop's ear—

and that "prince of cats" Tybalt, wanting to kill him on the spot but deterred by the host, and then the lovers' first exchange—

> ROMEO If I profane with my unworthiest hand
>   This holy shrine, the gentle fine is this,
>   My lips, two blushing pilgrims, ready stand
>   To smooth that rough touch with a tender kiss.
> JULIET Good pilgrim, you do wrong your hand too much,
>   Which mannerly devotion shows in this;
>   For saints have hands that pilgrims' hands do touch,
>   And palm to palm is holy palmers' kiss.
> ROMEO Have not saints lips, and holy palmers too?
> JULIET Ay, pilgrim, lips that they must use in prayer.
> ROMEO O, then, dear saint, let lips do what hands do;
>   They pray, grant thou, lest faith turn to despair.
> JULIET Saints do not move, though grant for prayers' sake.
> ROMEO Then move not, while my prayer's effect I take—

which is of course a sonnet, one sample of the artifice, after which Romeo learns her identity—

> Is she a Capulet?
> O dear account! my life is my foe's debt—

and Juliet his:

> NURSE His name is Romeo, and a Montague. . . .
> JULIET My only love sprung from my only hate!

So out of a swirling exposition we have for a time these two as move and object, and the barrier between—the enmity of the families—is backed by the Prince's decree. But they are lovers, a special variety of antagonist, and in what follows they unite to outwit the barrier; it transpires they are both the move; and Tybalt and Paris are in place to undo each, as two of the three surrogates for the true antagonist.

The second act is a single line from meeting to marriage, in five steps. One, Romeo invades the Capulet orchard to woo Juliet on a moonlit balcony, and finds himself engaged:

> JULIET If that thy bent of love be honourable,
>   Thy purpose marriage, send me word tomorrow,
>   By one that I'll procure to come to thee,
>   Where and what time thou wilt perform the rite.

Two, he takes himself off to Friar Laurence's cell:

> ROMEO   My heart's dear love is set
>   On the fair daughter of rich Capulet:
>   . . . . this I pray,
>   That thou consent to marry us today.
> FRIAR LAURENCE Holy Saint Francis, what a change is here!

Three, Juliet's nurse seeks out Romeo, is told by him

>   Bid her devise
>   Some means to come to shrift this afternoon;
>   And there she shall at Friar Laurence' cell
>   Be shrived and married—

and four, carries the message back to Juliet:

>   Hie you to church. . . .
>   I am the drudge, and toil in your delight;
>   But you shall bear the burthen soon at night.

Five, the lovers keep the rendezvous, and the friar announces

178

we will make short work;
For, by your leaves, you shall not stay alone
Till holy church incorporate two in one.

But on this single line is hung a variety of other fabrics
for our entertainment—the garrulous comedy of the
nurse, the good friar's philosophizing, the madcap banter
of Mercutio—and under all the playwright is plucking at
an invisible line, thematic. Romeo has apprised us of it
in his first misgiving, "some vile forfeit of untimely
death," the tragic fiat; and thereafter the playwright puts
the dread word in every mouth, both lovers'—

JULIET   The orchard walls are high and hard to climb,
   And the place death, considering who thou art,
   If any of my kinsmen find thee here. . . .
ROMEO   My life were better ended by their hate,
   Than death prorogued, wanting of thy love—

and the friar's—

Within the infant rind of this small flower
Poison hath residence, and medicine power. . . .
Two such opposed kings encamp them still
In man as well as herbs, grace and rude will;
And where the worser is predominant,
Full soon the canker death eats up that plant—

and Mercutio's—

Alas, poor Romeo, he is already dead; stabbed with a white
wench's black eye; shot through the ear with a love-song;
the very pin of his heart cleft with the blind bow-boy's
butt-shaft—

and Romeo's and the friar's again—

ROMEO   Do thou but close our hands with holy words,
   Then love-devouring death do what he dare,

It is enough I may but call her mine.

FRIAR LAURENCE   These violent delights have violent ends,
And in their triumph die; like fire and powder
Which as they kiss consume—

until we perceive that, as in *Macbeth*, the true antagonist
emerging is an abstraction; here, it is love-devouring
death. But this is the playwright's object, not the lovers'.

Somebody must act in its cause; the third act, heading
for the pivot, sweeps in from the first the two characters
so intended. In moves Tybalt, seeking a duel with Romeo,
finds it instead with the other hothead Mercutio, and
kills him; Romeo then challenges Tybalt—

Mercutio's soul
Is but a little way above our heads,
Staying for thine to keep him company—

and in turn kills him; he takes flight from the Prince,
whose move is to condemn him in absentia:

for that offence
Immediately we do exile him hence. . . .
Else, when he's found, that hour is his last.

Tybalt has undone Romeo. The nurse is once more go-
between, bearing the news to Juliet in her orchard and
her summons to Romeo hiding in the friar's cell. The
friar's solution is that Romeo flee to another city

till we can find a time
To blaze your marriage, reconcile your friends,
Beg pardon of the prince and call thee back
With twenty hundred thousand times more joy
Than thou went'st forth in lamentation—

a happy ending which the playwright now moves Paris
in to close off. Again wooing Juliet's parents, Paris wins

their consent to a wedding three days later. But the
lovers are already in Juliet's chamber for their night of
love; at dawn Romeo drops from the balcony, with
Juliet now prescient of the fiat—

> JULIET   O God! I have an ill-divining soul.
> Methinks I see thee, now thou art below,
> As one dead in the bottom of a tomb. . . .
> ROMEO   Dry sorrow drinks our blood—

and they part, maximally joined and separated: immediately the parents are moved in, the third surrogate for
the true antagonist, and the act builds to its curtain in a
family brawl—

LADY CAPULET   The gallant, young, and noble gentleman,
   The County Paris, at Saint Peter's Church,
   Shall happily make thee there a joyful bride.
JULIET   Now, by Saint Peter's Church, and Peter too,
   He shall not make me there a joyful bride. . . .
CAPULET   . . . . go with Paris to Saint Peter's Church,
   Or I will drag thee on a hurdle thither. . . .
JULIET   Good father, I beseech you on my knees. . . .
CAPULET   Hang thee, young baggage! . . . . it makes me
    mad:
   Day, night, hour, tide, time, work, play,
   Alone, in company, still my care hath been
   To have her match'd. . . .
   An you be mine, I'll give you to my friend;
   An you be not, hang, beg, starve, die in the streets. . . .
JULIET   O, sweet my mother, cast me not away! . . . .
LADY CAPULET   Talk not to me, for I'll not speak a word—

which leaves Juliet alone, undone by Paris:

> I'll to the friar, to know his remedy:
> If all else fail, myself have power to die.

So we have the third-act pivot, love against death, and the plunge begins.

It must reunite the lovers; that—with a farewell glance at Paris—is the unfinished business, but the promise is not simple. They live in a double play, a palimpsest of their own and the playwright's. In their play, each is the move and each the other's object; in the playwright's, both are the move, and the object is death. The plunge must keep both promises, and its contortions twice strain our good-will to believe.

The fourth act is all Juliet's. In her move to the friar's cell she encounters Paris briefly—

> PARIS   Poor soul, thy face is much abused with tears.
> JULIET   The tears have got small victory by that;
>   For it was bad enough before their spite—

and she is left with the friar, who has the next move:

> JULIET   Give me some present counsel; or, behold,
>   'Twixt my extremes and me this bloody knife
>   Shall play the umpire. . . .
> FRIAR LAURENCE   Hold, daughter: I do spy a kind of
>   hope. . . .
>   Thou hast the strength of will to slay thyself,
>   Then is it likely thou wilt undertake
>   A thing like death. . . .
> JULIET   O, bid me leap, rather than marry Paris,
>   From off the battlements. . . .
>   And I will do it without fear or doubt,
>   To live an unstain'd wife to my sweet love.
> FRIAR LAURENCE   Take you this vial, being then in bed,
>   And this distilled liquor drink thou off—

which will put her in a deathlike swoon for two and forty hours, till she awakens in the family tomb; Romeo, informed by letter, will carry her off. It is a somewhat kinky plan. The first contortion, it is not unrelated to character; Juliet is desperate—

> Give me, give me! O, tell me not of fear—

takes the vial home, plays the penitent for her parents, and in the solitude of her chamber, after much inner contradiction—

> What if it be a poison, which the friar
> Subtly hath minister'd to have me dead,
> Lest in this marriage he should be dishonour'd. . . .
> How if, when I am laid into the tomb,
> I wake before the time that Romeo
> Come to redeem me? there's a fearful point.
> Shall I not then be stifled in the vault. . . .
> Or, if I live. . . . shall I not be distraught,
> Environed with all these hideous fears?
> And madly play with my forefathers' joints?—

she drinks the potion:

> Romeo, I come! this do I drink to thee.

In the morning, amid the wedding preparations, the nurse coming to wake her cries the alarm—

> Lady! lady! lady!
> Alas, alas! Help, help! my lady's dead!
> O, well-a-day, that ever I was born!—

and the act ends on a wail of general lamentation, plus a bit of comedy by the company's clowns.

The fifth act turns to Romeo in exile, happy—

> If I may trust the flattering truth of sleep,
> My dreams presage some joyful news at hand—

until his servant brings him word of Juliet's death.

> BALTHASAR   Her body sleeps in Capels' monument,
>   And her immortal part with angels lives.
>   I saw her laid low in her kindred's vault,
>   And presently took post to tell it you. . . .
> ROMEO   Is it e'en so? then I defy you, stars!

And his move is to buy a forbidden poison for himself:

> APOTHECARY   Put this in any liquid you will,
>   And drink it off; and, if you had the strength
>   Of twenty men, it would dispatch you straight.
> ROMEO   There is thy gold, worse poison to men's souls,
>   Doing more murders in this loathsome world,
>   Than these poor compounds that thou mayst not sell:
>   I sell thee poison, thou has sold me none. . . .
>   Come, cordial and not poison, go with me
>   To Juliet's grave.

Back in the cell, Friar Laurence is visited by a monk who was to take his letter to Romeo; the plague has prevented its delivery. This instant plague, blown in from nowhere but the playwright's mind, is the bad luck which makes the tragedy, a second contortion related only to the fiat. The final scene is in the graveyard where Juliet that night sleeps; Paris comes in as mourner—

> Sweet flower, with flowers thy bridal bed I strew—

and retires from another torch; it is Romeo, come to force the tomb—

> Why I descend into this bed of death
> Is partly to behold my lady's face. . . .
> Thou detestable maw, thou womb of death,
> Gorged with the dearest morsel of the earth,
> Thus I enforce thy rotten jaws to open—

184

till Paris intervenes. They duel, and Romeo kills him. His dying request is to be buried with Juliet, and now, as in every great moment, the angel in our playwright opens his enormous wings:

ROMEO   O, give me thy hand,
   One writ with me in sour misfortune's book!
   I'll bury thee in a triumphant grave;
   A grave? O, no, a lantern. . . .
   For here lies Juliet, and her beauty makes
   This vault a feasting presence full of light. . . .
   . . . . O my love! my wife!
   Death, that hath suck'd the honey of thy breath,
   Hath had no power yet upon thy beauty:
   Thou art not conquer'd; beauty's ensign yet
   Is crimson in thy lips and in thy cheeks,
   And death's pale flag is not advanced there. . . .
   . . . . I still will stay with thee,
   And never from this palace of dim night
   Depart again: here, here will I remain
   With worms that are thy chamber-maids; O, here
   Will I set up my everlasting rest,
   And shake the yoke of inauspicious stars
   From this world-wearied flesh. . . .

It is enough to reconcile him—and almost us—to this omnivorous fellow, death. Romeo drinks the poison—

   Thus with a kiss I die—

and Juliet, waking to find his body fallen upon hers—

   O churl! drunk all, and left no friendly drop
   To help me after?—I will kiss thy lips;
   Haply some poison yet doth hang on them,
   To make me die with a restorative.
   Thy lips are warm. . . . O happy dagger!
   This is thy sheath; there rust, and let me die—

185

stabs herself; they have vaulted the barrier, into death.

Or, the barrier has become the bridge which joins them. In their play and in the playwright's, both, the master move and object have met, the lovers are reunited, in death, and only the barrier survives. It is now meaningless, keeps apart no one we care about, and when half the town pours in—

PRINCE   Where be these enemies? Capulet! Montague!
   See, what a scourge is laid upon your hate,
   That heaven finds means to kill your joys with love! . . . .
CAPULET   O brother Montague, give me thy hand—

it too goes down.

Death has been forced upon this pair; in a sense, the subject of this tragedy is tragedy, a first essay in the uses of death, and the playwright's hand shows. The form is in transition, the mature tragedies are yet to come. But it gives us most nakedly the other half of the answer to our question, What happens in its innards when a play is done?—and the answer is, as we should expect, the exact reverse of what the initial "happening" has begun.

The move is the microstructure. Comedy or tragedy, a play is done when the master move overcomes the barrier to find the master object, and *all three* are altered in such a way that no further move is possible. The plunge binds what the happening has loosed. This is the new equilibrium which ends the play, and instantly our skins tell us the heat is off; the six or seven minutes of explication which follow Juliet's suicide are like hours, intolerable.

Yet Portia has extended her play by an entire act, at a risk, and can Shylock not indeed found a party to reform the laws of Venice?—physically, yes. This is comedy, the equilibrium is conditional, where there's life there's will. But push this conflict of wills deep enough and Shylock must kill or be killed; we then pass from living dogs to dead lions. Death is the equilibrium which is absolute, the moveless sea from whose bourn no traveller returns, and this is tragedy.

22. *The Plunge, Tragic*

Only six years after these star-cross'd lovers were in print the 1603 quarto of *Hamlet* appeared; *Othello* seems to have been acted in 1604; *Lear* was definitely on the boards by 1606. With these three plays we are in the thick of the decade of great tragedies, and our own unfinished business is to look at what remains in each.

The problem created by the third-act pivot in *Hamlet* is simply put: it breaks the back of the play. For three acts we have watched Hamlet close in on a mystery. Now it is lifted, the King is guilty, and Hamlet makes two moves. One is the master move against the King, and he turns from it; the other is the move against his mother, and he completes it. The protagonist now has no move. With two acts to go, the playwright is stuck in a deadwater; he has a bifurcated play on his hands, an overt object in the King, a covert object in the mother, and no move in reserve against either. It is one of the conditions for an end.

The fact is, the play works; nobody walks out, and

the plunge—admittedly the weaker part of a masterpiece
—more than keeps things astir, it comes up with three of
the most memorable scenes in drama, and in the last moment unifies the two objects. The business left unfinished is the King and—we shall soon see its use—Polonius'
corpse. The crying need is a new move for Hamlet, and
the entire plunge is an engine to generate it; but he is
now dead weight, the playwright must first get him off
the stage.

The King has the move; he sends for Hamlet, who is
triumphantly manicky after the scene with his mother—

KING Now, Hamlet, where's Polonius?

HAMLET At supper.

KING At supper! where?

HAMLET Not where he eats, but where he is eaten; a certain convocation of politic worms are e'en at him. Your
worm is your only emperor for diet: we fat all creatures
else to fat us, and we fat ourselves for maggots: your fat
king and your lean beggar is but variable service, two
dishes, but to one table: that's the end.

KING Alas, alas! . . . . Where is Polonius?

HAMLET In heaven; send thither to see: if your messenger
find him not there, seek him i' the other place yourself—

and the King orders Rosencrantz and Guildenstern to
take him off to England; they bear a sealed letter calling
for his murder. En route, he passes Fortinbras and his
army on the march—

How all occasions do inform against me,
And spur my dull revenge! . . . . Now, whether it be
Bestial oblivion. . . . I do not know
Why yet I live to say, 'this thing's to do,'
Sith I have cause, and will, and strength, and means,
To do't. . . . while to my shame I see

189

> The imminent death of twenty thousand men,
> That for a fantasy and trick of fame
> Go to their graves like beds—

and tells us again his thoughts will "be bloody"; but bestial oblivion, of the inward barrier, is still between him and the King.

With the stage clear, the move now passes to subordinate characters. Enter Ophelia, mourning her father with ditties of death and betrayal in the mad scene, a dark mirror of Hamlet's breaking-point gaiety, and drifting away just as her brother Laertes storms in from France at the head of a rabble, also mirroring Hamlet in reverse detail:

LAERTES   O thou vile king,
   Give me my father!
QUEEN   Calmly, good Laertes.
LAERTES   That drop of blood that's calm proclaims me
   bastard;
   Cries cuckold to my father; brands the harlot
   Even here, between the chaste unsmirched brows
   Of my true mother.

The King leads Laertes away for a bit, to "commune with your grief." In the interval, sailors bring Horatio a letter—Hamlet has escaped and is on his way back—but here the 1603 text gives us, instead of a story-point, a scene in which Horatio delivers this news to the Queen; she condemns her husband—

> There's treason in his lookes
> That seem'd to sugar o're his villanie:
> But I will soothe and please him for a time—

and so becomes the accomplice of her son—

190

> Commend me
> A mothers care to him, bid him a while
> Be wary of his presence, lest that he
> Faile in that he goes about. . . . I take my leave,
> With thowsand mothers blessings to my sonne—

which keeps the promise of their bedchamber scene. The interval done, the King and Laertes come back reconciled, learn of Hamlet's escape, and plot a fencing-match in which Laertes will have a rapier not only unbated, but —it is Laertes' own scheme, quite out of character— dipped in poison. In the 1603 text, it is the King's scheme. In both texts, the King will also have ready a poisoned drink for Hamlet's refreshment. With this plot laid, they hear of Ophelia's drowning in a brook while she

> chanted snatches of old tunes,
> As one incapable of her own distress,

thus ending the fourth act with Laertes in fresh grief, doubly motivated.

The fifth act is the trap, then, into which Hamlet steps; both acts have been built on Polonius' corpse. Still without a move, indeed depleted after the triumph with his mother, Hamlet is seen haunting a graveyard, skull-obsessed—

Did these bones cost no more the breeding, but to play at loggats with 'em? . . . . Where be your gibes now? your gambols? your songs? your flashes of merriment? . . . . Now get you to my lady's chamber, and tell her, let her paint an inch thick, to this favour she must come—

when the funeral procession enters to inter Ophelia. Laertes leaps into the grave for a last embrace, with Hamlet in after him—

HAMLET   What is he whose grief
   Bears such an emphasis? . . . . This is I,
   Hamlet the Dane.
LAERTES   The devil take thy soul!—

and they grapple until parted:

HAMLET   I loved Ophelia: forty thousand brothers
   Could not, with all their quantity of love,
   Make up my sum. . . . Hear you, sir;
   What is the reason that you use me thus?
   I loved you ever—

and Laertes as surrogate antagonist is now an immediate
trigger for Hamlet's move to come. In the castle hall for
the final scene, Hamlet tells Horatio how he unsealed
the King's letter, substituted Rosencrantz's and Guildenstern's names, and escaped:

HORATIO   So Guildenstern and Rosencrantz go to't.
HAMLET   Why, man they did make love to this employ-
   ment;
   They are not near my conscience. . . .
HORATIO   Why, what a king is this!
HAMLET   Does it not, think'st thee, stand me now upon—
   He that hath kill'd my king, and whored my mother;
   Popp'd in between the election and my hopes;
   Thrown out his angle for my proper life,
   And with such cozenage—is 't not perfect conscience
   To quit him with this arm?

Here is a third motive, to revenge the attempt on his
own life; it issues in nothing but his consent to idle sport,
the King's fencing-match. Yet despite his anxiety—

HAMLET   But thou wouldst not think how ill all's here about
   my heart: but it is no matter.
HORATIO   Nay, good my lord—

HAMLET   It is but foolery; but it is such a kind of gain-
giving as would perhaps trouble a woman.
HORATIO   If your mind dislike any thing, obey it. I will
forestall their repair hither, and say you are not fit—

he has made his peace with whatever dreams death may
hold:

If it be now, 'tis not to come; if it be not to come, it will be
now; if it be not now, yet it will come; the readiness is
all. . . .

The whole court is in for the match, the King spices
Hamlet's poisoned cup with "an union" or great pearl,
and Laertes and Hamlet "play"; the first two hits are
Hamlet's, and the Queen takes up the cup.

QUEEN   The queen carouses to thy fortune, Hamlet.
HAMLET   Good, madam—
KING   Gertrude, do not drink.
QUEEN   I will, my lord; I pray you, pardon me. . . .
LAERTES   Have at you now!

Hamlet is wounded, with the unbated rapier, and in an
"incensed" exchange seizes it to pay Laertes back; now
the Queen falls.

In this moment the overt and covert levels fuse, and
the inward barrier becomes the bridge to the King:

LAERTES   I am justly kill'd with mine own treachery.
HAMLET   How does the queen?
KING   She swounds to see them bleed.
QUEEN   No, no, the drink, the drink,—O my dear Hamlet,—
The drink, the drink! I am poison'd.
HAMLET   O villainy! Ho! let the door be lock'd:
Treachery; seek it out.
LAERTES   It is here, Hamlet. . . .

> In thee is not half an hour of life;
> The treacherous instrument is in thy hand,
> Unbated and envenom'd. . . . thy mother's poison'd:
> I can no more: the king, the king's to blame.
> HAMLET The point envenom'd too!
> Then, venom, to thy work!

And he stabs the King. Is it to revenge his father?—no, nor even himself, he has not one dying word for any victim but his mother—

> KING O, yet defend me, friends; I am but hurt.
> HAMLET Here, thou incestuous, murderous, damned Dane,
> Drink off this potion: is thy union here?
> Follow my mother—

as he empties into the King's mouth the very cup that has poisoned her. It is his crowning move, duty and desire have at last found one object, in what is indeed a tragedy of revenge after all; but not of his father.

The play is done, move, barrier, object altered, a new equilibrium in effect; nothing remains but for young Fortinbras to rule honorably over it. The state survives, it is a form of redemption. So too in *Othello*, where the visiting nobles from Venice restore sanity and the survivor Cassio "rules in Cyprus." Tragedy looks for redemption to be tolerable. But in Elsinore the death of the hero is in the service of truth, and self-redemptive; *Othello* is grimmer meat.

Here the plunge poses another problem for the playwright, to move from intrigue to tragedy. Apart from the master promise, the questions still open are Iago's use of the handkerchief, his pledge to Othello to have Cas-

sio killed, and his management of both his dupes, Roderigo grown rebellious and his own wife; he has his hands
full. Iago is still writing this play, why is it not his? Because he is now inside the barrier—that is, inside Othello,
"I am your own forever"—and the play's center of interest is passing to Othello's inner contradiction.

Until the great third-act scene with Iago we saw
Othello monolithic, and so he began it:

> exchange me for a goat,
> When I shall turn the business of my soul
> To such exsufflicate and blown surmises,
> Matching thy inference. . . .
> Nor from mine own weak merits will I draw
> The smallest fear, or doubt of her revolt;
> For she had eyes, and chose me.

This allusion to his blackness, whose chief function in
the play is to open him to self-doubt, Iago exploited at
once.

IAGO   And when she seem'd to shake and fear your looks,
   She lov'd them most.
OTHELLO   And so she did.
IAGO   Why, go to, then;
   She that so young could give out such a seeming,
   To seel her father's eyes up close as oak—
   He thought 'twas witchcraft. . . .
OTHELLO   I do not think but Desdemona's honest. . . .
   And yet, how nature erring from itself—

at which point one famed actor lowering his hand from
his brow would stare at it—

IAGO   Ay, there's the point: as—to be bold with you—
   Not to affect many proposed matches
   Of her own clime, complexion, and degree. . . .

We then saw Othello alone in a flurry of conflicting moods—doubtful, resolute, credulous, proud, unbelieving—

> Why did I marry? . . . . If I do prove her haggard,
> Though that her jesses were my dear heart-strings,
> I'd whistle her off and let her down the wind
> To prey at fortune. Haply, for I am black
> And have not those soft parts of conversation. . . .
> She's gone; I am abus'd. . . . I had rather be a toad,
> And live upon the vapour of a dungeon,
> Than keep a corner in the thing I love
> For others' uses. . . .
> If she be false, O, then heaven mocks itself!
> I'll not believe 't—

which, with Iago's return, becomes an agony—

OTHELLO   Avaunt! be gone! thou hast set me on the rack:
   I swear 'tis better to be much abused
   Than but to know 't a little.
IAGO   How now, my lord!
OTHELLO   What sense had I of her stol'n hours of lust? . . .
   I saw 't not, thought it not, it harm'd not me:
   I slept the next night well, was free and merry;
   I found not Cassio's kisses on her lips—

and his wretched valediction—

>   O, now for ever
> Farewell the tranquil mind! farewell content!
> Farewell the plumed troop and the big wars
> That make ambition virtue! O, farewell,
> Farewell the neighing steed and the shrill trump,
> The spirit-stirring drum, the ear-piercing fife,
> The royal banner and all quality,
> Pride, pomp, and circumstance of glorious war!
> . . . . Othello's occupation's gone!—

is a leavetaking of psychic unity; from this moment on his wars will be in himself. And only so does he reclaim the play from Iago.

The fourth act is in three scenes: the first two are complex, interweaving intrigue and tragedy. Iago opens with the handkerchief—

IAGO But for the handkerchief—
OTHELLO By heaven, I would most gladly have forgot it:
Thou said'st—O, it comes o'er my memory,
As doth the raven o'er the infected house,
Boding to all—he had my handkerchief—

and with it teases Othello into a stammering fit:

OTHELLO What hath he said?
IAGO Faith, that he did—I know not what he did.
OTHELLO What? what?
IAGO Lie—
OTHELLO With her?
IAGO With her, on her; what you will.
OTHELLO Lie with her! lie on her! We say lie on her, when they belie her. Lie with her! zounds! that's fulsome! Handkerchief—confessions—handkerchief! . . . . I tremble at it. . . . It is not words that shakes me thus. Pish! Noses, ears and lips. Is 't possible?—Confess?—Handkerchief?—O devil!

The trance he falls into, which Iago terms epilepsy, marks the loss of himself; henceforth he is Iago's. Whose next move is to set Othello watching while he quizzes Cassio—ostensibly to

make him tell the tale anew,
Where, how, how oft, how long ago and when
He hath and is again to cope your wife—

only about his strumpet Bianca. Not the stratagem, which is flimsy enough, but Othello's inward breaking—the halves are past love and murder to come—is the heart of the scene:

IAGO   Did you perceive how he laughed at his vice?
OTHELLO   O Iago!
IAGO   And did you see the handkerchief? . . . .
OTHELLO   I would have him nine years a-killing. A fine woman! a fair woman! a sweet woman!
IAGO   Nay, you must forget that.
OTHELLO   Ay; let her rot, and perish, and be damned to-night; for she shall not live. . . . O, the world hath not a sweeter creature; she might lie by an emperor's side, and command him tasks.
IAGO   Nay, that's not your way.
OTHELLO   Hang her! I do but say what she is: so delicate with her needle: an admirable musician: O, she will sing the savageness out of a bear: of so high and plenteous wit and invention:—
IAGO   She's the worse for all this.
OTHELLO   O, a thousand thousand times: and then, of so gentle a condition!
IAGO   Ay, too gentle.
OTHELLO   Nay, that's certain: but yet the pity of it, Iago! O Iago, the pity of it, Iago!

Again Iago assigns the move—

IAGO   If you are so fond over her iniquity, give her patent to offend. . . .
OTHELLO   Get me some poison, Iago; this night I'll not expostulate with her, lest her body and beauty unprovide my mind again. . . .
IAGO   Do it not with poison, strangle her in her bed, even the bed she hath contaminated—

and the tragic decision is taken.

This play began as one of solitary will versus conjoined love, readable—or so I suggested—as narcissism
undoing our capacity to love. What is Othello's object
now?—at the end he will label himself

> An honourable murderer. . . .
> For nought did I in hate, but all in honour,

as much a "flattering unction" as his concern for society's good:

> Yet she must die, else she'll betray more men.

The "honour" he is so impassioned to avenge is self-love.
It is a treasuring of the very eminence which was the
barrier to Iago's frontal assault and is now the bridge
between them; working Othello from within, the narcissism which will undo both of these lovers is Iago's
will become Othello's honor. Here this play too bifur-
cates. On the fork which is intrigue, Iago turns Othello
loose and is free to tidy up the ends of his plot; on the
fork which is tragedy—a sub-play in itself—Othello is the
move, his love's death the object, and the barrier is his
inner contradiction. The intrigue will be fulfilled in the
fulfilment of the tragedy.

So this act turns toward the victims. In come the nobles visiting from Venice; Othello reading their letters is
so enraged by Desdemona's conversation—

LODOVICO   Is there division 'twixt my lord and Cassio?
DESDEMONA   A most unhappy one: I would do much
    To atone them, for the love I bear to Cassio.
OTHELLO   Fire and brimstone!
DESDEMONA   My lord?
OTHELLO   Are you wise?
DESDEMONA   What, is he angry?

LODOVICO May be the letter moved him;
   For, as I think, they do command him home,
   Deputing Cassio in his government.
DESDEMONA By my troth, I am glad on 't.
OTHELLO Indeed!
DESDEMONA My lord?
OTHELLO I am glad to see you mad.
DESDEMONA Why, sweet Othello?
OTHELLO Devil!—

that he strikes her, to the consternation of all; when he leaves, Lodovico asks whether his wits are "safe."

LODOVICO Is . . . this the nature
   Whom passion could not shake? . . . .
    IAGO He is much changed.

So far the first scene takes us; in the second, Othello pursues Desdemona to another room, and in accusing her is overcome—

OTHELLO Pray, chuck, come hither.
DESDEMONA What is your pleasure?
OTHELLO Let me see your eyes;
   Look in my face. . . .
DESDEMONA Alas, the heavy day! Why do you weep?
   Am I the motive of these tears, my lord?—

sliding deeper than Job into the chasm between loving and killing:

OTHELLO Had it pleased heaven
   To try me with affliction, had they rain'd
   All kinds of sores and shames on my bare head,
   Steep'd me in poverty to the very lips,
   Given to captivity me and my utmost hopes,
   I should have found in some place of my soul
   A drop of patience. . . . O thou weed,

Who art so lovely fair and smell'st so sweet
That the sense aches at thee, would thou hadst ne'er been
   born!
DESDEMONA   Alas, what ignorant sin have I committed? . . . .
OTHELLO   Are not you a strumpet?
DESDEMONA   No, as I am a Christian. . . .
OTHELLO   What, not a whore?
DESDEMONA   No, as I shall be saved.
OTHELLO   It 't possible?
DESDEMONA   O, heaven forgive us!—

yes, all—

   OTHELLO   I cry you mercy, then:
      I took you for that cunning whore of Venice
      That married with Othello.

And he leaves Desdemona stunned, with Iago's wife.

   EMILIA   . . . how do you, my good lady?
   DESDEMONA   Faith, half asleep.

Good Iago enters, and Desdemona turns to him for help:

DESDEMONA   Am I that name, Iago?
IAGO   What name, fair lady?
DESDEMONA   Such as she says my lord did say I was.
EMILIA   He call'd her whore. . . .
   What place? what time? what form? what likelihood?
   The Moor's abused by some most villainous knave,
   Some base notorious knave. . . .
IAGO   You are a fool; go to.
DESDEMONA   O good Iago,
   What shall I do to win my lord again?
   Good friend, go to him. . . .
IAGO   Go in, and weep not; all things shall be well.

It is the cruelest thing he says. The intrigue resumes with
Roderigo, in to berate Iago for gulling him of money

with no advancement of his wooing; and Iago gulls him again—

RODERIGO The jewels you have had from me to deliver to Desdemona would half have corrupted a votarist. . . . I will make myself known to Desdemona: if she will return me my jewels, I will give over my suit. . . . if not, assure yourself I will seek satisfaction of you. . . .

IAGO Why, now I see there's mettle in thee, and even from this instant do build on thee a better opinion than ever before. Give me thy hand, Roderigo—

proposing one further act of valor which will earn him a night with Desdemona: with Cassio deputed governor, Othello will take Desdemona away—

IAGO . . . . unless his abode be lingered here by some accident: wherein none can be so determinate as the removing of Cassio.

RODERIGO How do you mean, removing of him?

IAGO Why, by making him uncapable of Othello's place; knocking out his brains.

RODERIGO And that you would have me do?

IAGO . . . . I will be near to second your attempt. . . .

The simple scene which concludes the act returns us to the tragedy; it is a melancholy lyric, all Desdemona's, as she prepares herself for bed in her wedding sheets.

The fifth act, the same night, has two scenes; the first consummates the intrigue, the second the tragedy. The intrigue finds Iago lurking in a street while Roderigo ambushes Cassio:

> Now, whether he kill Cassio,
> Or Cassio him, or each do kill the other,
> Every way makes my gain.

202

In the fracas Roderigo is wounded; Iago "from behind" wounds Cassio, is interrupted by the arrival of others, and kills Roderigo for an assassin; as a gratuity he lays the conspiracy on the strumpet Bianca, and has her arrested. It is his last clever move:

> This is the night
> That either makes me or fordoes me quite.

The tragedy finds Desdemona asleep in her bed as Othello approaches, and we are at the edge of the absolute:

OTHELLO   Put out the light, and then put out the light:
 If I quench thee, thou flaming minister,
 I can again thy former light restore,
 Should I repent me; but once put out thy light,
 Thou cunning'st pattern of excelling nature,
 I know not where is that Promethean heat
 That can thy light relume.

And, loving to the last, he kisses her; she wakes.

DESDEMONA   Will you come to bed, my lord?
OTHELLO   Have you pray'd tonight, Desdemona?
DESDEMONA   Ay, my lord.
OTHELLO   If you bethink yourself of any crime
 Unreconciled as yet to heaven and grace,
 Solicit for it straight.
DESDEMONA   Alas, my lord, what may you mean by that?
OTHELLO   . . . . I would not kill thy soul.
DESDEMONA   Talk you of killing?
OTHELLO   Ay, I do.
DESDEMONA   Then heaven have mercy on me! . . . .
OTHELLO   Think on thy sins.
DESDEMONA   They are loves I bear to you.
OTHELLO   Ay, and for that thou diest.
DESDEMONA   That death's unnatural that kills for loving—

but "it is the cause" of the play, loving and killing;
Othello accuses her again, she calls for Cassio as witness—

OTHELLO   No, his mouth is stopp'd;
  Honest Iago hath ta'en order for 't. . . .
DESDEMONA   Alas, he is betray'd and I undone!
OTHELLO   Out, strumpet! weep'st thou for him to my face?
DESDEMONA   . . . . Kill me tomorrow; let me live tonight!
OTHELLO   Nay, if you strive—
DESDEMONA   But half an hour!
OTHELLO   Being done, there is no pause.
DESDEMONA   But while I say one prayer!
OTHELLO   It is too late—

and he smothers her. In a tradition begun it seems in the
playwright's time, Othello, forced to a second attempt—

        Not dead? . . . .
    I would not have thee linger in thy pain.
    So, so—

now uses his dagger; it makes credible Desdemona's re-
vival for a dying word when Emilia runs in.

    EMILIA   O, who hath done this deed?
    DESDEMONA   Nobody; I myself. Farewell:
      Commend me to my kind lord. . . .
    OTHELLO   She's like a liar gone to burning hell;
      'Twas I that kill'd her.

The two forks rejoin here; Emilia cries for help, and all
including Iago are in to hear her tell the truth about the
handkerchief; Iago stabs her and flees, but is caught, and
Othello must face the horror of himself.

    Let it go all. . . .
    Here is my journey's end, here is my butt
    And very sea-mark of my utmost sail.

.... O ill-starr'd wench!
Pale as thy smock! when we shall meet at compt,
This look of thine will hurl my soul from heaven,
And fiends will snatch at it. Cold, cold, my girl!
.... Whip me, ye devils,
From the possession of this heavenly sight:
Blow me about in winds, roast me in sulphur,
Wash me in steep-down gulfs of liquid fire.
O Desdemona! Desdemona! dead!

He has two moves left; the first is his attempt to kill Iago
—the master encounter—and he fails.

IAGO   I bleed, sir, but not kill'd.
OTHELLO   I am not sorry neither, I'ld have thee live;
    For, in my sense, 'tis happiness to die . . .
    O fool! fool! fool! . . . .
LODOVICO   Your power and your command is taken off,
    And Cassio rules in Cyprus.

The second is to kill himself—

OTHELLO   Soft you; a word or two before you go.
    I have done the state some service, and they know 't;
    No more of that. I pray you, in your letters,
    When you shall these unlucky deeds relate,
    Speak of me as I am. . . .
    Perplex'd in the extreme; of one whose hand,
    Like the base Indian, threw a pearl away
    Richer than all his tribe—

and he succeeds, breathing his last upon Desdemona's
lips:

                    . . . no way but this,
          Killing myself, to die upon a kiss.

And Iago lives, the personification of will.

LODOVICO Look on the tragic loading of this bed;
This is thy work: the object poisons sight;
Let it be hid.

Move, object, barrier, all wrecked, the play closes on this tableau of unredeemed waste. "I am glad that I have ended my revisal of this dreadful scene," wrote that arch-enemy of cant, Samuel Johnson, "it is not to be endured." Romeo too dies upon the body of his beloved, but in union; Hamlet dies, but with his ends achieved. No such effort is made to reconcile us to these deaths, they are as wanton as man himself.

Yet a grimmer landscape is ahead, in *Lear*. The other tragedies are shot through with humor, lovers begin happily in a golden light, even the villains are engaging —Tybalt is beautiful, Hamlet's uncle is jovial, Iago has charm—but not under the lowering sky of Lear's land; its villains are gorgons and its one vein of humor, the Fool sprinkling his sour jokes, vanishes as the third-act pivot sounds its pedalpoint:

All dark and comfortless.

This is Gloucester blind, to which Kent in the final scene adds one word—

all's cheerless, dark, and deadly—

and hardly a scene in between but voices the theme of general doom; it arises out of the experience here, and not as in *Romeo and Juliet* by fiat. But there is fiat, as we shall see when the play brings us to its glimpse of salvation.

We left its chief characters scattered in the storm, one

old man psychotic, the other gouged of his eyes, and both homeless; Regan, with her wounded husband, is preparing to fight off an invasion by Cordelia; Edmund is riding with Goneril back to her husband; Kent is ministering to Lear in disguise, and Edgar is hiding on the moors as a mad beggar. The confrontations we have been promised are multiple. The war must be fought; Lear must come to terms with his cast-off daughter Cordelia, and Gloucester with his fugitive son Edgar; their bad seeds, Goneril, Regan, Edmund, must come to fruition, whatever it is; Edgar and Kent must unveil themselves, and Edgar must force an accounting with his bastard half-brother. It is an extraordinarily convoluted problem, and the plunge—which in *Othello* took five scenes—will here take ten, and skimp on all but Lear.

The fourth act picks up Edgar on the heath, cheering himself that

> The lamentable change is from the best;
> The worst returns to laughter—

when his father Gloucester is led in by an old tenant; and at once the pedalpoint is renewed:

GLOUCESTER   Thy comforts can do me no good at all;
   Thee they may hurt.
OLD MAN   . . . you cannot see your way.
GLOUCESTER   I have no way and therefore want no eyes;
   I stumbled when I saw. . . .
EDGAR (*aside*)   O gods! Who is 't can say, 'I am at the worst?'
   I am worse than e'er I was. . . .
GLOUCESTER   As flies to wanton boys, are we to the gods;
   They kill us for their sport.

Lamenting his lost son, Gloucester hires the "naked fellow" to lead him to Dover cliff, from which he will "no leading need"—

OLD MAN   Alack, sir, he is mad.
GLOUCESTER   'Tis the times' plague, when madmen lead the
    blind—

and son and father both are moved to the forlorn love—

EDGAR *(aside)*   Bless thy sweet eyes, they bleed. . . .
GLOUCESTER   Here, take this purse, thou whom the heavens'
    plagues
    Have humbled to all strokes. . . .
    So distribution should undo excess,
    And each man have enough—

which is emerging as counterpoint to the play's woe; it is a replay of Lear's tardy "I have ta'en too little care of this," the first note of saving grace.

Four brief scenes catch up the other characters, notably Cordelia, out of the play since its opening. We see Edmund only momentarily in this act—having launched its moves, he is dispensable—when he returns Goneril to her husband Albany, and leaves; she prefers him.

> O, the difference of man and man!
> To thee a woman's services are due:
> My fool usurps my body.

Which opens a new promise. Albany's move is to attack her—

> O Goneril!
> You are not worth the dust which the rude wind
> Blows in your face—

adding his voice on Lear's behalf to the pedalpoint:

208

> It will come,
> Humanity must perforce prey on itself,
> Like monsters of the deep.

Goneril thinks him a "moral fool" who would do better
to attack Cordelia's army—

> Where's thy drum?
> France spreads his banners in our noiseless land—

but they are interrupted by a messenger, Regan's husband is dead of his wound, and the promise of the war
breaks over their nuptial enmity. We shift now to Dover
to meet gentle Cordelia again; Kent has smuggled news
to her—

> patience and sorrow strove
> Who should express her goodliest. You have seen
> Sunshine and rain at once: her smiles and tears
> Were like a better way—

and her move is to send searchers out after Lear, who is
shunning her for shame.

> CORDELIA   . . . why, he was met even now
> As mad as the vex'd sea; singing aloud,
> Crown'd with. . . . all the idle weeds that grow
> In our sustaining corn. . . .
> No blown ambition doth our arms incite,
> But love, dear love—

which is the promise of their meeting; it is held in suspense. In Gloucester's castle, Oswald turns up with a
letter from his mistress Goneril to Edmund; he is off to
the war, and Regan charges Oswald with her own
message—

> My lord is dead; Edmund and I have talk'd,
> And more convenient is he for my hand
> Than for your lady's—

which is another promise; the bad seeds are coming to-gether.

The last scenes of the act deliver its main substance, the fathers and their wronged children. Edgar, leading his to Dover to fling himself from the cliff, fibs that they are at its edge—

> EDGAR   Why I do trifle thus with his despair
>   Is done to cure it.
> GLOUCESTER   O you mighty gods!
>   This world I do renounce, and in your sights
>   Shake patiently my great affliction off. . . .
>   . . . . If Edgar live, O bless him!—

and the old man leaps, survives his little fall, and resolves that

>   henceforth I'll bear
>   Affliction till it do cry out itself
>   'Enough, enough,' and die. . . .
>   EDGAR   Bear free and patient thoughts—

an episode whose purpose, apart from its dubious the-atricality, is to insist on life however blind. In wanders Lear, crowned with crazy weeds, and the two old dere-licts of both stories at last meet in this travesty of royal power—

> LEAR   Give the word.
> EDGAR   Sweet marjoram.
> LEAR   Pass.
> GLOUCESTER   I know that voice. . . . Is 't not the king?
> LEAR   Ay, every inch a king:

When I do stare, see how the subject quakes.
I pardon that man's life. What was thy cause?
Adultery?—

but neither has a move, it is all lamentation; Lear delves
into the lusts dead in him—

The wren goes to 't, and the small gilded fly
Does lecher in my sight. . . .
Behold yond simpering dame,
Whose face between her forks presages snow,
That minces virtue and does shake the head
To hear of pleasure's name;
The fitchew, nor the soiled horse, goes to 't
With a more riotous appetite.
Down from the waist they are Centaurs,
Though women all above:
But to the girdle do the gods inherit,
Beneath is all the fiends';
There's hell, there's darkness, there is the sulphurous pit,
Burning, scalding, stench, consumption—

equating the places of birth and damnation, and the two
men join in the pedalpoint:

GLOUCESTER   O, let me kiss that hand!
LEAR   Let me wipe it first; it smells of mortality.
GLOUCESTER   O ruin'd piece of nature! This great world
    Shall so wear out to nought.

Pathetic, gay, wrathful, Lear is all inner contradiction
here, of saving grace—

Thou rascal beadle, hold thy bloody hand!
Why dost thou lash that whore? Strip thine own back;
Thou hotly lust'st to use her in that kind
For which thou whip'st her. . . .
None does offend, none, I say none—

and suffering—

> LEAR   . . . we came crying hither:
>   Thou know'st, the first time that we smell the air,
>   We waul and cry. . . .
> GLOUCESTER   Alack, alack the day!
> LEAR   When we are born, we cry that we are come
>   To this great stage of fools—

and "mortality"—

>   And when I have stol'n upon these sons-in-law,
>   Then, kill, kill, kill, kill, kill, kill!

And when Cordelia's move of searchers now finds him, he knows it himself:

> LEAR   Let me have a surgeon;
>   I am cut to the brains.
> GENTLEMAN   You shall have any thing.

Alone, Gloucester and Edgar close in on their own reconciliation; but Edgar is holding himself incognito for a more climactic moment.

> GLOUCESTER   Now, good sir, what are you?
> EDGAR   A most poor man. . . .
>   Who, by the art of known and feeling sorrows,
>   Am pregnant to good pity.

But Oswald enters, another of mortality's party, with a grisly line—

>   Most happy!
>   That eyeless head of thine was first fram'd flesh
>   To raise my fortunes—

and in his move to kill Gloucester is himself slain by Edgar; on him is Goneril's letter inviting Edmund to murder her husband and occupy his bed.

The act comes to focus on the master encounter between Lear and Cordelia. In her tent, she watches over
him in his convalescent sleep, and speaks the pity of the
counterpoint—

> Was this a face
> To be expos'd against the warring winds?
> To stand against the deep dread-bolted thunder? . . . .
> With this thin helm? Mine enemy's dog,
> Though he had bit me, should have stood that night
> Against my fire—

and Lear wakes out of the long night of all four acts:

LEAR   You do me wrong to take me out o' the grave;
>   . . . . I am bound
> Upon a wheel of fire, that mine own tears
> Do scald like molten lead. . . .

DOCTOR   He's scarce awake: let him alone awhile.

LEAR   Where have I been? Where am I? Fair day-
light? . . . .

CORDELIA   O, look upon me, sir,
> And hold your hands in benediction o'er me. . . .

LEAR   Pray, do not mock me:
> I am a very foolish fond old man,
> Fourscore and upward, not an hour more nor less;
> And, to deal plainly,
> I fear I am not in my perfect mind.
> . . . . I am mainly ignorant
> What place this is, and all the skill I have
> Remembers not these garments, nor I know not
> Where I did lodge last night. Do not laugh at me;
> For, as I am a man, I think this lady
> To be my child Cordelia.

CORDELIA   And so I am, I am.

LEAR   Be your tears wet? yes, faith. I pray, weep not:
> If you have poison for me, I will drink it.

I know you do not love me; for your sisters
Have, as I do remember, done me wrong:
You have some cause, they have not.
CORDELIA   No cause, no cause.

The "great rage is kill'd in him," the barrier is down, suffering has made it their bridge; move and object have met, and the Lear version is done. The play will be completed by the forces unleashed by Edmund. Lear's last humble words in the scene are

Pray you now, forget and forgive: I am old and foolish—

and the act ends with "this day's battle" imminent.

The third-act pivot divided these characters into successes and failures. The successes have become murderers, the failures are groping their way to love; that is the glimpse of salvation; the play in its close is tilting toward the same redeeming ethic we saw in Isabella, Portia, Prospero, the mercies of love on our sins. But this time the playwright's heart is not in it. The last scene snatches the glimpse from us; the total arc of the structure is as cruel as Iago's moment, "All things shall be well."

The battle in the fifth act is the moment of fiat. It is preceded by a scene wherein Edgar, delivering to Goneril's husband her letter plotting his murder, pledges to "prove" it in single fight; this move against Edmund will be the star combat of the act, and the war dwindles to a preliminary instant. Here it is entire:

EDGAR   . . . take the shadow of this tree
For your good host; pray that the right may thrive:
If ever I return to you again,
I'll bring you comfort.

214

GLOUCESTER   Grace go with you, sir!
           Exit Edgar. Alarum and retreat within.
           Re-enter Edgar.
EDGAR   Away, old man; give me thy hand; away!
    King Lear hath lost, he and his daughter ta'en.

In both the "historie" and old play on which the Lear
half is based, the right does thrive; Cordelia's army wins
and a happy ending follows. That her move fails here—
structurally bizarre, the marines come to the rescue and
are defeated?—is the playright's choice. But hardly free,
after the agony with which he has charged both stories
a happy outcome would be mockery. In Edgar's tag to
the battle—

          Men must endure
    Their going hence, even as their coming hither:
    Ripeness is all—

the insistence is still on enduring.

    The final scene is all disintegration. Lear and Cordelia
are led in as prisoners, and the old king like Gloucester
renounces the world:

LEAR   Come, let's away to prison:
    We two alone will sing like birds i' the cage:
    When thou dost ask me blessing, I'll kneel down
    And ask of thee forgiveness: so we'll live,
    And pray, and sing, and tell old tales, and laugh
    At gilded butterflies, and hear poor rogues
    Talk of court news; and we'll talk with them too,
    Who loses and who wins, who's in, who's out;
    And take upon 's the mystery of things,
    As if we were God's spies. . . .
EDMUND   Take them away.
LEAR   . . . . Have I caught thee?

He that parts us shall bring a brand from heaven,
And fire us hence like foxes.

Edmund is that he, and his move is to order them hanged;
so unified are the two stories now it seems illogical to no
one that the villain of the one kills the heroine of the
other. In come the victors, with Goneril and Regan
squabbling over Edmund, until Albany breaks in—

> Edmund, I arrest thee
> On capital treason; and, in thy attaint,
> This gilded serpent—

with Goneril's letter in hand; Edmund is to stand trial by
combat, and Regan is led away—

> REGAN   Sick, O sick!
> GONERIL *(aside)*   If not, I'll ne'er trust medicine—

to die of her sister's poison. The trumpet is sounded, Edgar appears vizored to keep the promise of his master encounter, and in hand-to-hand combat with that "most
toad-spotted traitor" Edmund, slays him; now he un-
vizors. Goneril flees, to stab herself offstage. Edmund
dying speaks for the bad seeds—

> I was contracted to them both: all three
> Now marry in an instant—

in the only score for morality, and Edgar tells of another
death, Gloucester's—

> his flaw'd heart. . . .
> Burst smilingly—

unseen because we must see Lear's. Kent now is in, to say
farewell because the "strings of life" are cracking in him
too. Nothing is left but Lear and Cordelia; and when he

enters with her dead in his arms, the book of doomsday is almost closed.

LEAR   Howl, howl, howl, howl! O, you are men of stones:
  Had I your tongues and eyes, I'd use them so
  That heaven's vaults should crack. She's gone for ever!
  I know when one is dead and when one lives;
  She's dead as earth. . . .
KENT   Is this the promised end?
EDGAR   Or image of that horror?

And in the very moment that Albany as the state voices the comfort which is custom, Lear gives him the lie—

ALBANY   All friends shall taste
  The wages of their virtue, and all foes
  The cup of their deservings. . . .
  LEAR   And my poor fool is hang'd! No, no, no life!
  Why should a dog, a horse, a rat, have life,
  And thou no breath at all? Thou'lt come no more,
  Never, never, never, never, never!—
  Pray you, undo this button—

and his heart breaks.

What move now?—hardly a breath remains. Of the eleven principals who began this tragedy, two survive; move, barrier, object are annihilated in both versions. No play is bleaker than this, in which one word—old, old, old—tolls like a knell, and over Lear's body Kent speaks the last blessing:

              O, let him pass! he hates him
    That would upon the rack of this tough world
    Stretch him out longer.

But the plunge has left behind it the theme even of superannuation. It has dug below comforting—Cordelia's beachhead of "love, dear love" has served only to deliver her body for an ending that tells us, whatever moral law exists, it is not discernible on the human level. In the other tragedies, death is an end; here the entire play is an image of dying, and comes to rest on a bedrock of eschatology.

It is not the playwright's last word; still to come are the late "romances," *Pericles, Cymbeline, The Tempest, The Winter's Tale,* in which children lost and given up for dead are found again, and all have a second chance. But these may be as cynical as serene. And of this galaxy of words we have voyaged in—so exhaustive of man's experience it is incomprehensible as the work of a single hand—who would dare cite one as Shakespeare's last? We can say only what our frailty would like to think, that his leavetaking is Cymbeline's—

Pardon's the word to all.

23. *Afterword*

The theatre is always alive, which means, changing; it has changed even in the few years since I stopped teaching my students, and almost four centuries have washed over these plays. A natural question is, How much of their structure is still valid, that is, usable by us?—which I generously leave to every playwright to answer for himself. I do owe my answer to an earlier question I left hanging, Does the structure—not its contents, we have abstracted from the most varied contents of these plays a certain geometry they have in common, and I mean the geometry—imply an image of man?

As a mirror of man the social animal, it reflects the obvious. The equilibrium of society, always uneasy, will be broken into by some unforeseen event, and the disruption will breed factions pursuing different ends in a struggle which concludes either in some comedy of compromise or in tragic destruction. No news there. Survivors who like Fortinbras inherit the state machinery are characters about whom we know next to nothing, and the new equilibrium we accept is founded upon that ignorance. There is always a next play to be written, and the testimony of the structure as a reiterated artifact is anti-utopian; only the struggle is eternal, which men have known since long before Ecclesiastes.

About man as an individual, the structure is less obvious; may we make a further game of it?—we will find in it something which took Hegel, whom I have not read, another two centuries to formulate and Freud, whom I have, three. Let us take another minute, and play with it as a model of our inner life.

As such, it intimates that the equilibrium of the mind, always uneasy, is periodically broken into by a "happening"; the disequilibrium releases energies which have been lurking in the tensions of a lifetime antecedent. What in the structure we call "exposition" is what modern psychiatry calls the case-history, and its function is identical, to explore in the present the data of the past in order to alter the future. Disequilibrium is unpleasant, and the energized mind makes a "move" toward some object which promises relief, that is, alteration; the "scene" is the record of that effort. In the outer world it brings me into conflict with others, will against will, but in my inner world "will against will" means one part of the self moving against another. Thus our interest quickens when characters like Angelo must deal with inner conflict; but even the external opposition of his lust and Isabella's virtue is familiar to each of us as an internal war. In their chain of scenes the alteration effected in one scene delivers them onto a larger battlefield for another—which is the story of our inner lives too. The "spring at the center" then is the individual's life-quest for the reconciliation of his deepest opposites in a new equilibrium which will end inner contradiction, when no further move is possible or needed. One word for this is death; another is God, and religious doctrine may be seen as a kind of communal drama which takes death itself as an antagonist to be confronted. The "barrier" to such psychic unity is an impediment within—a given, in our present game, and players may pick any first cause, contradictory prototypes of parents, or the opposite functions of the hemispheres of the brain, or original sin—which each of us struggles lifelong to overcome. In this struggle toward unity we create the scenes of our personal drama, we create our character, we create in part the other characters around us, we create our "theme"—in two words, we create the "intervening matter" which is the body of our life and which we experience as its unique identity.

The structure then is the story of our lives, and I think it is not entirely a game.

We are hypothecating one man's mind. Is there in fact such a man?—yes, he wrote the plays. All the contradictions we worked through in them were alive in his mind, and are alive again in any mind that takes them in as spectator. Which brings us once more to the mystery of the creative gift, and its meaning to us as audience; but if the father of psychoanalysis himself said it "must lay down its arms" in the face of that mystery, I am not the one to take them up again. I am content to note that this structure is, like the microscope, an *invention*. It enables the playwright to descend into his own underworld of contradictions, and loose pairs of them at each other in a violent mating whose offspring is some resolution that acknowledges both; that resolution is his temporary conquest, a bringing of some unity out of some opposites, and as spectators we share the conquest.

I said that one principle is at work in the structure, the move of human will against barriers. That such a move is possible is an article of faith implicit in it; what happens to the structure when man's image of himself begins to leak that faith?

The historical fact is that, adumbrated by the Greeks but not brought to its ultimate shaping even by Shakespeare's immediate predecessors, this structure has dominated western theatre-writing until our time. By the onset of this century, the philosophers had announced that God was dead, the astronomers that man was a bug, the economists that his ideals were class exploitation, the psychologists that he was an unwitting victim of his own unconscious, and the physicists that the real world was an illusion; some people began to lose confidence in themselves. The history of playwriting in the twentieth century opens with Chekhov, who modified this invention most expressively, conveying the aura of missed lives —his theme—by omitting most of the climactic confrontations, relegating them to the intermissions, and creating thus a wistful world of ineffectual people. Those plays inaugurated a process of whittling away at the three-hundred-year-old structure, until the later catastrophes of power in our time—two world wars, the Holocaust, the bomb on Hiroshima—left in their wake another devastation, a sense among many intellectuals of total impotence. And in the avant-garde drama which celebrated it, human will and this structure are equally vestigial.

But the theatre is alive, and changing; that generation too is dying out, and the playwrightless theatre is no longer in good health. If I had students now I could bring them the work of their own contemporaries who have gone to school with the realists of an earlier decade, and teach this structure from their plays. Like human will, it is perhaps not quite exhausted.

Index

ANTONY AND CLEOPATRA, 115–20, 148

AS YOU LIKE IT, 47, 49–52, 54, 148, 155

THE COMEDY OF ERRORS, 148

CORIOLANUS, 75, 148

CYMBELINE, 218

HAMLET, 6, 9–10, 12, 15–20, 22, 24, 25, 43–44, 52, 53, 54, 69, 71, 121–48, 149, 188–94, 206, 219

HENRY IV, First Part, 44–46, 52, 54

JULIUS CAESAR, 75, 148

KING LEAR, 6–7, 10–12, 91–112, 150, 188, 206–18

MACBETH, 73, 89–90, 114–15, 148, 149, 180

Index

MEASURE FOR MEASURE, 6–7, 10, 12, 25–42, 69, 87, 114, 148, 214, 220

THE MERCHANT OF VENICE, 7–8, 52, 77–86, 87–88, 93, 149, 150, 161–72, 174–75, 186–87, 214

A MIDSUMMER-NIGHT'S DREAM, 47–49, 54

OTHELLO, 52, 56–67, 72–73, 113–14, 188, 194–206, 207

PERICLES, 218

RICHARD II, 52, 73–74

RICHARD III, 88–89, 114

ROMEO AND JULIET, 7, 49, 71, 177–86, 206

THE TAMING OF THE SHREW, 74–75, 86, 144, 148

THE TEMPEST, 7, 13–15, 71, 114, 148, 150, 151–61, 173–74, 214

TWELFTH NIGHT, 148

THE WINTER'S TALE, 148, 218

William Gibson

has published poetry, plays, fiction, and auto-
biography; he is co-author with Margaret Bren-
man, a psychoanalyst, of two grown sons.
Shakespeare's Game is his first and last book as a
critic.

4096